SRA SPECTRUM MATH

FIFTH EDITION

red

Thomas J. Richards
Author

A Division of The McGraw·Hill Companies

Columbus, Ohio

Photo Credits
22, Ronnie Kaufman/Corbis-Stock Market; **80,** Doug
Martin; **90,** Robert Brenner/PhotoEdit; **114,** Doug Martin;
122, David Young-Wolff/PhotoEdit; **136,** Jeff Zaruba/
Tony Stone Images; **158,** Tony Freeman/PhotoEdit.

www.sra4kids.com

SRA/McGraw-Hill

A Division of The McGraw-Hill Companies

Send all inquiries to:
SRA/McGraw-Hill
8787 Orion Place
Columbus, OH 43240-4027

Printed in the United States of America.

ISBN 0-07-572332-8

3 4 5 6 7 8 9 MAZ 07 06 05 04

Contents

RED BOOK PRETESTS
Readiness Check

Add.

```
    4          8        2 0       3 1       8 6       7 6
  +5         +7       +4 0      +5 2        +3      +1 7
```

```
    7        2 0       1 3
    6        4 0       2 5       4 0 0     6 4 2     7 0 2
  +5       +3 0      +4 1      +3 0 0    +3 4 5    +1 4 6
```

Subtract.

```
    9        1 0       1 5       4 0       6 8       5 6
  -3         -6        -7      -3 0      -2 3      -2 6
```

```
  6 7        9 1       5 3       6 0     1 8 4     5 6 7
 -3 0       -1 6      -4 7      -2 3      -6 2     -1 4 0
```

Write the next three numbers.

23, 24, 25, _____ , _____ , _____

87, 88, 89, _____ , _____ , _____

137, 138, 139, _____ , _____ , _____

Count by 10.

30, 40, 50, _____ , _____ , _____ , _____ , _____

400, 410, 420, _____ , _____ , _____ , _____ , _____

170, 180, 190, _____ , _____ , _____ , _____ , _____

Ring the fraction that tells how much is blue.

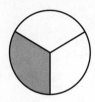   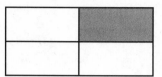

$\frac{1}{2}$ $\frac{1}{3}$ $\frac{1}{4}$ $\frac{1}{2}$ $\frac{1}{3}$ $\frac{1}{4}$ $\frac{1}{2}$ $\frac{1}{3}$ $\frac{1}{4}$

Write the time for each clock.

_____ : _____   _____ : _____   _____ : _____

How long is each object?

_____ centimeters   _____ inches

Solve each problem.

Mick has 346 pennies.

Matt has 213 pennies.

How many pennies do
they have in all?

Ms. Smith had 367 dollars.

She spent 132 dollars.

How many dollars does she
have left?

RED BOOK PRETESTS
Addition Facts (Pretest 1)

	a	*b*	*c*	*d*	*e*	*f*	*g*	*h*
1.	3 +1	8 +2	1 +6	4 +7	6 +3	2 +8	4 +5	7 +9
2.	6 +4	1 +8	3 +9	2 +1	5 +0	0 +2	9 +1	3 +2
3.	2 +7	6 +9	4 +8	9 +3	2 +2	8 +0	0 +4	7 +1
4.	5 +2	8 +3	1 +5	7 +8	6 +2	4 +6	5 +4	9 +4
5.	2 +3	9 +0	4 +3	2 +9	1 +1	8 +8	3 +5	5 +7
6.	8 +9	3 +3	9 +5	6 +6	3 +8	0 +6	7 +3	2 +6
7.	7 +7	4 +1	3 +6	8 +7	0 +0	9 +8	9 +2	7 +5
8.	2 +4	0 +3	5 +8	2 +5	1 +9	1 +0	5 +9	8 +4
9.	6 +7	3 +4	9 +9	0 +7	8 +5	7 +4	5 +6	3 +7
10.	9 +7	8 +6	5 +5	7 +6	6 +8	6 +5	4 +9	9 +6

RED BOOK PRETESTS
Addition Facts (Pretest 2)

	a	*b*	*c*	*d*	*e*	*f*	*g*	*h*
1.	8 +2	7 +0	0 +1	1 +1	6 +4	5 +2	4 +9	2 +7
2.	1 +0	6 +3	3 +0	2 +3	7 +1	8 +1	6 +5	1 +9
3.	0 +5	1 +2	6 +6	3 +5	9 +5	5 +7	7 +6	3 +8
4.	4 +2	6 +8	8 +5	2 +6	5 +8	9 +8	0 +0	4 +4
5.	7 +2	9 +7	0 +8	4 +7	7 +9	5 +9	3 +3	5 +4
6.	1 +3	9 +0	2 +2	5 +1	7 +7	6 +0	8 +6	9 +4
7.	4 +8	9 +3	1 +4	2 +9	9 +2	8 +3	7 +3	0 +9
8.	2 +0	2 +8	8 +4	4 +0	8 +7	9 +1	4 +3	5 +5
9.	8 +9	5 +6	6 +1	1 +7	4 +6	7 +5	9 +9	6 +7
10.	3 +9	9 +6	7 +8	5 +3	6 +9	8 +8	7 +4	3 +7

RED BOOK PRETESTS
Subtraction Facts (Pretest 1)

	a	*b*	*c*	*d*	*e*	*f*	*g*	*h*
1.	11 −3	8 −4	5 −5	12 −3	2 −1	10 −9	4 −3	11 −9
2.	10 −5	3 −3	6 −3	11 −4	7 −6	10 −6	9 −2	12 −4
3.	16 −7	9 −0	5 −4	13 −7	10 −2	15 −9	8 −8	14 −5
4.	13 −8	4 −2	7 −7	12 −9	2 −0	17 −9	6 −1	11 −7
5.	18 −9	9 −8	6 −4	11 −5	3 −1	15 −7	9 −9	10 −8
6.	12 −6	8 −7	3 −2	13 −9	10 −4	14 −6	7 −5	12 −5
7.	15 −8	8 −3	9 −5	12 −8	8 −6	16 −9	5 −3	12 −7
8.	14 −7	7 −1	6 −5	11 −6	4 −1	10 −7	1 −1	10 −3
9.	13 −4	0 −0	8 −0	16 −8	9 −7	14 −9	6 −6	13 −6
10.	17 −8	9 −6	7 −4	15 −6	11 −2	13 −5	9 −3	14 −8

RED BOOK PRETESTS
Subtraction Facts (Pretest 2)

	a	*b*	*c*	*d*	*e*	*f*	*g*	*h*
1.	4 −2	1 3 −7	3 −2	1 0 −1	6 −5	8 −1	1 4 −5	1 0 −7
2.	8 −2	1 2 −5	6 −3	1 0 −8	2 −1	1 1 −9	1 4 −8	1 1 −2
3.	4 −0	1 1 −3	9 −1	1 5 −6	5 −0	7 −1	1 3 −8	1 0 −9
4.	6 −4	1 3 −9	1 −0	9 −2	7 −3	1 2 −4	1 5 −7	5 −4
5.	0 −0	1 2 −3	8 −4	1 4 −6	8 −5	1 0 −4	1 6 −9	1 1 −6
6.	9 −9	1 0 −2	3 −2	1 5 −9	5 −1	1 2 −9	1 4 −9	1 0 −3
7.	7 −5	1 2 −7	7 −0	1 4 −7	7 −2	1 1 −4	1 6 −7	1 1 −5
8.	4 −4	1 3 −6	5 −2	1 6 −8	9 −4	1 0 −5	1 3 −4	6 −0
9.	8 −3	1 2 −6	1 −1	1 8 −9	4 −3	1 2 −8	1 4 −6	1 3 −5
10.	9 −6	1 1 −7	8 −8	1 7 −8	6 −2	1 0 −6	1 7 −9	1 5 −8

RED BOOK PRETESTS
Multiplication Facts (Pretest 1)

	a	*b*	*c*	*d*	*e*	*f*	*g*	*h*
1.	2 ×2	6 ×3	0 ×1	3 ×2	8 ×0	1 ×1	7 ×1	8 ×4
2.	7 ×4	3 ×0	8 ×3	2 ×1	5 ×1	3 ×6	2 ×5	6 ×2
3.	3 ×7	5 ×5	8 ×6	6 ×0	4 ×9	9 ×1	7 ×2	4 ×3
4.	8 ×5	2 ×4	7 ×5	4 ×1	8 ×2	6 ×5	7 ×8	1 ×9
5.	4 ×0	8 ×1	9 ×3	5 ×6	3 ×8	2 ×9	5 ×7	9 ×2
6.	7 ×9	6 ×4	4 ×8	7 ×3	6 ×9	9 ×4	2 ×6	8 ×7
7.	1 ×3	9 ×5	5 ×3	8 ×8	4 ×5	0 ×7	3 ×4	7 ×6
8.	3 ×5	9 ×0	2 ×7	7 ×7	5 ×8	9 ×6	2 ×0	6 ×6
9.	9 ×9	1 ×8	6 ×8	0 ×0	9 ×7	0 ×5	3 ×9	8 ×9
10.	4 ×6	9 ×8	2 ×8	4 ×7	1 ×6	6 ×7	3 ×3	5 ×9

RED BOOK PRETESTS
Multiplication Facts (Pretest 2)

	a	*b*	*c*	*d*	*e*	*f*	*g*	*h*
1.	2 ×2	6 ×4	4 ×1	7 ×7	1 ×0	2 ×9	0 ×2	1 ×4
2.	5 ×0	3 ×1	8 ×3	3 ×9	0 ×9	9 ×6	7 ×3	4 ×8
3.	1 ×2	4 ×9	6 ×3	7 ×2	5 ×7	1 ×5	2 ×8	8 ×2
4.	8 ×4	9 ×5	4 ×2	2 ×3	6 ×9	4 ×7	4 ×3	5 ×6
5.	2 ×4	7 ×1	3 ×3	6 ×2	9 ×4	5 ×1	6 ×8	7 ×6
6.	7 ×4	1 ×1	5 ×8	8 ×5	7 ×0	0 ×8	6 ×1	9 ×3
7.	3 ×8	9 ×7	5 ×2	2 ×6	3 ×4	8 ×9	7 ×5	6 ×7
8.	8 ×6	5 ×4	4 ×6	9 ×2	1 ×7	8 ×1	4 ×4	3 ×5
9.	6 ×5	7 ×8	9 ×9	0 ×0	3 ×7	5 ×5	2 ×5	8 ×8
10.	9 ×1	4 ×5	8 ×7	6 ×6	9 ×8	7 ×9	2 ×7	5 ×9

RED BOOK PRETESTS
Division Facts (Pretest 1)

	a	b	c	d	e	f	g
1.	$7\overline{)7}$	$4\overline{)24}$	$9\overline{)18}$	$3\overline{)18}$	$8\overline{)32}$	$6\overline{)12}$	$2\overline{)8}$
2.	$8\overline{)0}$	$1\overline{)9}$	$5\overline{)15}$	$2\overline{)16}$	$7\overline{)21}$	$5\overline{)0}$	$8\overline{)8}$
3.	$3\overline{)15}$	$8\overline{)40}$	$7\overline{)28}$	$4\overline{)20}$	$7\overline{)63}$	$3\overline{)21}$	$9\overline{)36}$
4.	$7\overline{)14}$	$5\overline{)20}$	$6\overline{)6}$	$2\overline{)18}$	$6\overline{)24}$	$1\overline{)2}$	$2\overline{)10}$
5.	$8\overline{)24}$	$5\overline{)10}$	$4\overline{)28}$	$9\overline{)45}$	$1\overline{)8}$	$5\overline{)45}$	$8\overline{)48}$
6.	$5\overline{)40}$	$6\overline{)30}$	$1\overline{)6}$	$5\overline{)5}$	$9\overline{)0}$	$8\overline{)16}$	$4\overline{)4}$
7.	$9\overline{)54}$	$1\overline{)5}$	$7\overline{)56}$	$6\overline{)18}$	$4\overline{)16}$	$6\overline{)54}$	$3\overline{)6}$
8.	$7\overline{)35}$	$3\overline{)12}$	$2\overline{)0}$	$8\overline{)56}$	$2\overline{)12}$	$6\overline{)0}$	$7\overline{)49}$
9.	$4\overline{)0}$	$8\overline{)64}$	$5\overline{)35}$	$4\overline{)32}$	$3\overline{)24}$	$1\overline{)3}$	$6\overline{)36}$
10.	$6\overline{)42}$	$9\overline{)9}$	$4\overline{)8}$	$1\overline{)0}$	$9\overline{)63}$	$4\overline{)12}$	$5\overline{)25}$
11.	$3\overline{)9}$	$2\overline{)14}$	$9\overline{)72}$	$7\overline{)42}$	$2\overline{)4}$	$8\overline{)72}$	$1\overline{)1}$
12.	$9\overline{)81}$	$6\overline{)48}$	$4\overline{)36}$	$2\overline{)6}$	$5\overline{)30}$	$1\overline{)4}$	$3\overline{)27}$

RED BOOK PRETESTS
Division Facts (Pretest 2)

	a	*b*	*c*	*d*	*e*	*f*	*g*
1.	2)‾2‾	4)‾1 2‾	3)‾9‾	6)‾2 4‾	8)‾4 8‾	3)‾6‾	8)‾0‾
2.	6)‾3 0‾	9)‾3 6‾	7)‾1 4‾	2)‾4‾	5)‾5‾	5)‾4 0‾	7)‾6 3‾
3.	1)‾7‾	5)‾0‾	5)‾4 5‾	9)‾4 5‾	4)‾8‾	1)‾9‾	8)‾5 6‾
4.	3)‾3‾	4)‾1 6‾	7)‾5 6‾	5)‾3 5‾	8)‾8‾	4)‾4‾	9)‾5 4‾
5.	7)‾0‾	3)‾1 2‾	8)‾6 4‾	6)‾3 6‾	7)‾2 1‾	2)‾6‾	4)‾3 6‾
6.	9)‾2 7‾	2)‾8‾	6)‾1 8‾	9)‾0‾	6)‾5 4‾	1)‾0‾	6)‾1 2‾
7.	6)‾0‾	4)‾2 0‾	8)‾4 0‾	1)‾1‾	8)‾7 2‾	3)‾1 5‾	5)‾3 0‾
8.	9)‾1 8‾	5)‾2 5‾	7)‾4 9‾	4)‾2 4‾	3)‾2 4‾	9)‾6 3‾	2)‾1 0‾
9.	3)‾0‾	9)‾9‾	6)‾4 8‾	2)‾1 4‾	6)‾6‾	1)‾6‾	8)‾1 6‾
10.	3)‾1 8‾	7)‾3 5‾	1)‾4‾	9)‾7 2‾	4)‾2 8‾	2)‾1 2‾	7)‾4 2‾
11.	1)‾8‾	8)‾3 2‾	5)‾2 0‾	5)‾1 0‾	2)‾1 8‾	6)‾4 2‾	5)‾1 5‾
12.	8)‾2 4‾	3)‾2 1‾	9)‾8 1‾	2)‾1 6‾	7)‾2 8‾	3)‾2 7‾	4)‾3 2‾

RED BOOK PRETESTS
Mixed Facts Pretest

Add, subtract, multiply, or divide. Watch the signs.

	a	*b*	*c*	*d*	*e*	*f*	*g*
1.	7 +6	8 +3	14 −9	9 ×9	13 −6	7 ×9	5)‾4‾5
2.	3 ×4	9 +7	11 −7	6 ×4	9 +9	10 −6	6)‾4‾2
3.	15 −8	5 ×5	4 ×7	12 −5	7 +8	5 +4	8)‾6‾4
4.	7 +5	16 −8	4 +8	14 −7	9 ×0	6 ×6	7)‾3‾5
5.	7 ×7	9 +5	17 −8	5 ×6	8 +9	17 −9	9)‾6‾3
6.	15 −6	13 −9	5 +6	8 +5	9 ×6	4 ×8	7)‾5‾6
7.	6 +6	3 ×9	8 ×8	7 +7	18 −9	10 −5	8)‾4‾0
8.	7 ×8	16 −9	11 −3	2 +9	8 +8	6 ×3	9)‾8‾1

Add, subtract, multiply, or divide. Watch the signs.

	a	b	c	d
9.	5 2 +6	3 8 −5	1 8 ×6	9)5 4
10.	7 6 −1 2	8)3 5	6 5 +7	5 0 ×7
11.	1 8 ×4 7	6 3 +2 4	9)4 0	3 2 −1 7
12.	6)1 6 8	4 7 ×5 6	5 8 4 −2 3	6 0 3 +7 2
13.	5 7 8 +4 9	3 7 2 −6 8	3 6 ×4 7	7)8 6 1
14.	7 0 5 −1 8 3	9 0 ×5 6	8)3 6 2 6	8 9 7 +2 6 8

PROBLEM SOLVING STRATEGIES

Choose the Operation

Harold saw seven geese flying in the sky. His friend Vicky saw eight more geese near a pond. How many geese did they see in all?

___Add___ to find how many in all.

They saw ___15___ geese.

Add to find how many in all.

7 geese flying
+ 8 geese near a pond
15 geese in all

Solve each problem.

SHOW YOUR WORK

1. Erin saw a robin's nest in the tree outside her bedroom window. On Monday there were five eggs in the nest. On Tuesday, she noticed that two eggs were missing. How many eggs were in the nest on Tuesday?

   _____ to find the difference.

   There were _____ eggs in the nest on Tuesday.

2. Last year there were 28 children in Juan's class. This year there are 3 fewer children in his class. How many children are in Juan's class this year?

   _____ to find how many fewer.

   There are _____ children in Juan's class this year.

3. At the zoo Wally saw 20 monkeys in a tree. He also saw 26 monkeys on the ground. How many monkeys did Wally see?

   _____ to find how many in all.

   Wally saw _____ monkeys.

PROBLEM SOLVING STRATEGIES
Draw a Picture

Kerry is setting up six tables in the school cafeteria. How many different ways can she arrange the tables in rows of equal length?

Kerry can have one row of _____6_____ tables.

Kerry can have two rows of _____3_____ tables.

Kerry can have three rows of _____2_____ tables.

Kerry can have six rows of _____1_____ table.

There are _____4_____ ways to arrange six tables.

Use x for each table. Draw all the ways you could arrange the tables.

1 row: 2 rows:
x x x x x x   x x x
                x x x

3 rows: 6 rows:
x x   x
x x   x
x x   x
                x
                x
                x

Solve each problem.

```
  ┌─────────────────┐
  │ SHOW YOUR WORK  │
  └─────────────────┘
         ▽
```

1. Lorie planted a flower garden. The first row has five flowers. Each row after that has one less flower. How many flowers did Lorie plant?

   The second row will have _____ flowers.

   Lorie planted _____ flowers in all.

---

2. Mr. Lange's class lines up in a certain order. Roy, Troy, and Joy lead the line, but not necessarily in that order. Joy stands in front of Roy. Troy does not stand next to Joy. Who is first in line?

   Since Troy does not stand next to Joy, he must stand next to _____.

   _____ is first in line.

PROBLEM SOLVING STRATEGIES
Look for a Pattern

At her first basketball game, Leah made one basket. At her second basketball game, Leah made three baskets. At her third game, she made five baskets. If the pattern continues, how many baskets will Leah make at her fifth game?

Leah will make ____9____ baskets at her fifth game.

Look for a pattern. The pattern is +2.

Game:	1st	2nd	3rd
Baskets:	1	3	5

Fourth Game: 5 + 2 = 7
Fifth Game: 7 + 2 = 9

Leah made nine baskets at her fifth game.

Solve each problem.

SHOW YOUR WORK

1. Mickey is making a pattern on a piece of grid paper. He put one dot in the first column. He put three dots in the second column, six dots in the third column, and ten in the fourth. If he continues with the same pattern, how many dots will Mickey put in the sixth column?

   Mickey should put _____ dots in column 6.

---

2. Lupita is putting beads in cups. She put two beads in the first cup and five beads in the second cup. If she put eight beads in the third cup, how many beads did she put in the fourth and fifth cups?

   Lupita put _____ beads in the fourth cup and _____ beads in the fifth cup.

PROBLEM SOLVING STRATEGIES
Guess and Check

Kane has 6 pets. Some are birds and some are dogs. In all, they have a total of 16 legs. How many birds and dogs does Kane have?

A bird has ____2____ legs.

A dog has ____4____ legs.

Kane has ____4____ birds and ____2____ dogs.

Guess possible numbers of each animal. Check to see if the total number of legs is 16.

Guess: 3 birds and 3 dogs
Legs: 2 + 2 + 2 = 6 bird legs
            4 + 4 + 4 = 12 dog legs
Total Legs: 6 + 12 = 18
                        Incorrect.

Guess: 4 birds and 2 dogs
Legs: 2 + 2 + 2 + 2 = 8 bird legs
            4 + 4 = 8 dog legs
Total Legs: 8 + 8 = 16
                        Correct.

Solve each problem.

1. Ellis is thinking of two numbers. They each have two digits. The sum of the two numbers is 100. The first number is 20 more than the second number. What are the two numbers Ellis is thinking of?

   The two numbers Ellis is thinking of are _____ and _____.

2. Nell has eight coins that total $0.38. She has at least one dime, one nickel, and one penny. How many of each coin does she have?

   Nell has _____ dimes, _____ nickels, and _____ pennies.

3. There were 60 children waiting in line to see a movie. They were told to get into four equal lines. How many children were in each line?

   There should be _____ children in each line.

PROBLEM SOLVING STRATEGIES
Identify Missing Information

Bill has tickets for himself and a friend to see a movie. He plans to meet his friend for dinner at 5:00 and then go to the movie. They take 45 minutes for dinner, and the drive to the theater takes another 10 minutes. Will they be able to make the movie on time?

Not enough information

Missing information: the time the movie starts

Add the times to find the time they could arrive at the theater.

5:00 + 45 minutes = 5:45
5:45 + 10 minutes = 5:55

Bill and his friend will be at the theater by 5:55.

The time the movie starts is missing.

Solve each problem.

SHOW YOUR WORK

1. Kuri spent $200 on a CD and a CD player. What was the exact amount that she spent on the CD?

_____

Missing information: _____

_____

2. Leon has a four-digit address. These four digits have a sum of 15. The first two digits are 1 and 4. What is Leon's four-digit address?

_____

Missing information: _____

_____

3. Gloria has two dollar bills, three quarters, five nickels, and seven dimes. How many gel pens can she buy?

_____

Missing information: _____

PROBLEM SOLVING STRATEGIES
Make a Table

Ricky needs three stamps for each sports magazine he mails. He plans to mail eight sports magazines. How many stamps will Ricky need?

Ricky will need ___24___ stamps.

Make a table.

Number of Sports Magazines	Number of Stamps
1	3
2	6
3	9
4	12
5	15
6	18
7	21
8	24

Solve each problem.

SHOW YOUR WORK

1. There are 60 girls planning to help with a cookie sale for charity. Each group of 10 girls will bake and decorate 15 dozen cookies. How many cookies will be made?

   Sixty girls will bake _____ dozen cookies.

2. Michael makes and sells kite tails. He can make eight kite tails from 5 yards of fabric. How many kite tails can he make from 35 yards of fabric?

   Thirty-five yards of fabric will make _____ kite tails.

PROBLEM SOLVING STRATEGIES
Work a Simpler Problem

For Saturday's concert, the school band sold 39 child tickets for $3 and 27 adult tickets for $5. How much money did they collect?

Now, solve the problem using these steps.

$39 \times 3 = 117$
$27 \times 5 = 135$
Add: $117 + 135 = \underline{252}$ dollars

Solve a simpler problem using easier numbers to see which operations will help.

Assume there are 40 child tickets and 30 adult tickets.

$40 \times 3 = 120$
$30 \times 5 = 150$
Add: $120 + 150 = 270$

Solve each problem.

SHOW YOUR WORK

1. A train carrying new animals to the zoo traveled 22 miles in half an hour. At that rate, how far would the train travel in three hours?

   The train travels _____ miles in three hours.

---

2. Mrs. Davis bought three balls for $6.05 each. How much did she spend?

   Mrs. Davis spent _____.

---

3. When the food was ready, the microwave oven began beeping. It beeped 11 times in 20 seconds. How many times would the oven beep in 5 minutes?

   [Hint: 60 seconds = 1 minute]

   The microwave would beep _____ times in five minutes.

PROBLEM SOLVING STRATEGIES
Work Backward

Anja is in a science class that is making a bridge out of craft sticks. Her teacher gave her 300 craft sticks. Later, her teacher gave another 200 sticks to someone else in her class. The teacher now has 400 craft sticks left. How many craft sticks did Anja's teacher originally have?

Anja's teacher originally had ____900____ craft sticks.

Start with what she had left and work backward.

Craft sticks she has now:	400
+ what she gave to a student:	200
	600
+ what she gave to Anja:	300
	900

Anja's teacher originally had 900 craft sticks.

Solve each problem.

SHOW YOUR WORK

1. Robert solved five math problems before dinner. After dinner he solved six more problems. He now has four problems left to solve. How many problems did Robert have for math homework?

Robert had _____ homework problems.

2. Glen went to the "Everything Under 50¢" store. He spent 25¢ on a comic book, 15¢ on a plastic football, and 38¢ on a pair of sunglasses. When he left the store he had $1.00 left. How much money did Glen have before he went into the store?

Glen had _____ before he went into the store.

3. Fred is 2 inches taller than Ann. Ann is 3 inches taller than Sue. Sue is 48 inches tall. How tall is Fred?

Fred is _____ inches tall.

CHAPTER 1 PRETEST
Addition and Subtraction (basic facts)

Add.

	a	b	c	d	e	f
1.	2 +8	7 +5	9 +4	5 +5	6 +8	8 +9
2.	4 +7	8 +5	6 +4	9 +9	1 +9	8 +7
3.	8 +8	9 +5	6 +7	7 +3	4 +8	9 +3
4.	3 +8	6 +6	9 +2	7 +7	9 +7	6 +9

Subtract.

	a	b	c	d	e	f
5.	10 − 3	12 − 8	15 − 6	14 − 5	18 − 9	16 − 8
6.	13 − 5	12 − 4	16 − 7	10 − 2	11 − 7	14 − 6
7.	10 − 5	12 − 6	11 − 2	15 − 7	17 − 9	10 − 8
8.	12 − 5	10 − 1	13 − 4	17 − 8	11 − 3	10 − 6
9.	12 − 9	15 − 8	16 − 9	11 − 5	13 − 6	14 − 7

Solve each problem.

1. Two adults and two children are playing. How many people are playing?

There are _____ adults.

There are _____ children.

There are _____ people playing.

1.

2. The Durhams played soccer for one hour and then played baseball for two hours. How many hours did they play in all?

They played soccer for _____ hour.

They played baseball for _____ hours.

They played _____ hours in all.

2.

3. The Durhams' house has five bedrooms in all. There are two bedrooms downstairs. The rest of the bedrooms are upstairs. How many bedrooms are upstairs?

There are _____ bedrooms in all.

There are _____ bedrooms downstairs.

There are _____ bedrooms upstairs.

3.

Lesson 1 Addition Facts through 9

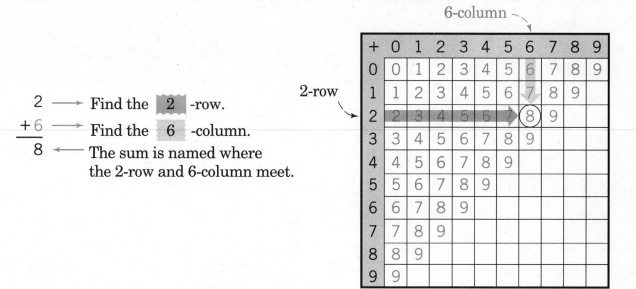

2 — → Find the **2**-row.

+6 — → Find the **6**-column.

8 ← The sum is named where the 2-row and 6-column meet.

Add.

	a	b	c	d	e	f	g	h
1.	2 +4	3 +1	1 +2	7 +0	0 +4	1 +4	5 +2	3 +3
2.	2 +0	6 +3	4 +4	3 +0	5 +3	1 +6	0 +5	8 +1
3.	2 +6	1 +0	1 +5	2 +2	3 +2	2 +1	5 +4	1 +7
4.	9 +0	5 +1	0 +3	4 +1	4 +5	1 +8	8 +0	4 +3
5.	0 +0	2 +3	7 +1	0 +9	4 +2	0 +2	0 +7	1 +1
6.	2 +7	0 +1	6 +2	0 +6	1 +3	6 +1	6 +0	7 +2

Lesson 2 Subtraction Facts through 9

6-column

–	0	1	2	3	4	5	6	7	8	9
0	0	1	2	3	4	5	6	7	8	9
1	1	2	3	4	5	6	7	8	9	
2	2	3	4	5	6	7	8	9		
3	3	4	5	6	7	8	9			
4	4	5	6	7	8	9				
5	5	6	7	8	9					
6	6	7	8	9						
7	7	8	9							
8	8	9								
9	9									

$\begin{array}{r} 8 \\ -6 \\ \hline 2 \end{array}$ → Find 8 in
→ the 6 -column.
← The difference is named in the ▨ at the end of this row.

Subtract.

	a	b	c	d	e	f	g	h
1.	$\begin{array}{r}5\\-4\\\hline\end{array}$	$\begin{array}{r}3\\-2\\\hline\end{array}$	$\begin{array}{r}7\\-7\\\hline\end{array}$	$\begin{array}{r}1\\-0\\\hline\end{array}$	$\begin{array}{r}8\\-2\\\hline\end{array}$	$\begin{array}{r}9\\-7\\\hline\end{array}$	$\begin{array}{r}4\\-3\\\hline\end{array}$	$\begin{array}{r}6\\-1\\\hline\end{array}$
2.	$\begin{array}{r}7\\-2\\\hline\end{array}$	$\begin{array}{r}2\\-2\\\hline\end{array}$	$\begin{array}{r}7\\-6\\\hline\end{array}$	$\begin{array}{r}8\\-7\\\hline\end{array}$	$\begin{array}{r}9\\-3\\\hline\end{array}$	$\begin{array}{r}9\\-8\\\hline\end{array}$	$\begin{array}{r}4\\-1\\\hline\end{array}$	$\begin{array}{r}6\\-0\\\hline\end{array}$
3.	$\begin{array}{r}0\\-0\\\hline\end{array}$	$\begin{array}{r}7\\-1\\\hline\end{array}$	$\begin{array}{r}3\\-0\\\hline\end{array}$	$\begin{array}{r}6\\-6\\\hline\end{array}$	$\begin{array}{r}4\\-2\\\hline\end{array}$	$\begin{array}{r}6\\-2\\\hline\end{array}$	$\begin{array}{r}9\\-5\\\hline\end{array}$	$\begin{array}{r}8\\-6\\\hline\end{array}$
4.	$\begin{array}{r}9\\-9\\\hline\end{array}$	$\begin{array}{r}8\\-4\\\hline\end{array}$	$\begin{array}{r}9\\-1\\\hline\end{array}$	$\begin{array}{r}7\\-5\\\hline\end{array}$	$\begin{array}{r}7\\-4\\\hline\end{array}$	$\begin{array}{r}6\\-5\\\hline\end{array}$	$\begin{array}{r}2\\-0\\\hline\end{array}$	$\begin{array}{r}1\\-1\\\hline\end{array}$
5.	$\begin{array}{r}3\\-1\\\hline\end{array}$	$\begin{array}{r}9\\-4\\\hline\end{array}$	$\begin{array}{r}7\\-3\\\hline\end{array}$	$\begin{array}{r}5\\-2\\\hline\end{array}$	$\begin{array}{r}5\\-1\\\hline\end{array}$	$\begin{array}{r}6\\-4\\\hline\end{array}$	$\begin{array}{r}4\\-4\\\hline\end{array}$	$\begin{array}{r}8\\-1\\\hline\end{array}$
6.	$\begin{array}{r}5\\-5\\\hline\end{array}$	$\begin{array}{r}2\\-1\\\hline\end{array}$	$\begin{array}{r}5\\-0\\\hline\end{array}$	$\begin{array}{r}8\\-3\\\hline\end{array}$	$\begin{array}{r}9\\-0\\\hline\end{array}$	$\begin{array}{r}6\\-3\\\hline\end{array}$	$\begin{array}{r}7\\-0\\\hline\end{array}$	$\begin{array}{r}5\\-3\\\hline\end{array}$

Lesson 3   Addition Facts through 12

7-column

+	0	1	2	3	4	5	6	7	8	9
0	0	1	2	3	4	5	6	7	8	9
1	1	2	3	4	5	6	7	8	9	10
2	2	3	4	5	6	7	8	9	10	11
3	3	4	5	6	7	8	9	10	11	12
4	4	5	6	7	8	9	10	11	12	
5	5	6	7	8	9	10	11	12		
6	6	7	8	9	10	11	12			
7	7	8	9	10	11	12				
8	8	9	10	11	12					
9	9	10	11	12						

$5 \longrightarrow$ Find the **5**-row.

$+7 \longrightarrow$ Find the **7**-column.

$\overline{12} \longleftarrow$ The sum is named where the 5-row and 7-column meet.

5-row

Add.

	a	b	c	d	e	f
1.	6 +5	7 +3	2 +7	8 +4	9 +2	6 +3
2.	8 +2	3 +9	3 +5	5 +2	6 +4	5 +5
3.	5 +3	9 +3	6 +6	3 +7	4 +7	9 +1
4.	5 +7	8 +1	5 +6	2 +8	2 +5	7 +5
5.	3 +4	4 +5	4 +6	2 +9	8 +3	4 +8
6.	2 +6	1 +9	3 +8	7 +1	7 +4	6 +2

Lesson 3 Problem Solving

Solve each problem.

1. Andy played two games today. He played nine games yesterday. How many games did he play in all? | **1.**

   Andy played _____ games today.

   Andy played _____ games yesterday.

   He played _____ games in all.

2. Jenna rode her bicycle 8 kilometers yesterday. She rode 4 kilometers today. How many kilometers did she ride in all? | **2.**

   Jenna rode _____ kilometers yesterday.

   Jenna rode _____ kilometers today.

   Jenna rode _____ kilometers in all.

3. Paul hit the ball seven times. He missed four times. How many times did he swing at the ball? | **3.**

   Paul hit the ball _____ times.

   Paul missed the ball _____ times.

   Paul swung at the ball _____ times.

4. There were four people in a room. Six more people came in. How many people were in the room then? | **4.**   **5.**

   _____ people were in a room.

   _____ more people came in.

   _____ people were in the room then.

5. Heather and Justin each read six books. How many books did they read in all?

   They read _____ books in all.

Lesson 4 Subtraction Facts through 12

4-column

−	0	1	2	3	4	5	6	7	8	9
0	0	1	2	3	4	5	6	7	8	9
1	1	2	3	4	5	6	7	8	9	10
2	2	3	4	5	6	7	8	9	10	11
3	3	4	5	6	7	8	9	10	11	12
4	4	5	6	7	8	9	10	11	12	
5	5	6	7	8	9	10	11	12		
6	6	7	8	9	10	11	12			
7	7	8	9	10	11	12				
8	8	9	10	11	12					
9	9	10	11	12						

11 ⟶ Find 11 in

−4 ⟶ the 4 -column.

7 ⟵ The difference is named in the ▨ at the end of this row.

Subtract.

	a	b	c	d	e	f
1.	1 1 −7	1 0 −4	1 0 −8	1 2 −9	8 −5	1 1 −2
2.	1 0 −1	1 1 −8	7 −4	1 1 −6	1 2 −3	9 −6
3.	1 2 −7	1 0 −7	9 −3	1 1 −9	1 2 −4	1 0 −5
4.	8 −6	1 2 −8	9 −5	1 0 −6	1 1 −5	8 −8
5.	1 2 −6	1 0 −9	9 −8	7 −6	1 1 −4	9 −7
6.	1 0 −2	7 −3	1 0 −3	1 2 −5	8 −3	1 1 −3

Lesson 4 Problem Solving

Solve each problem.

1. There were 12 nails in a box. David used 3 of them. How many nails are still in the box?

   _____ nails were in a box.

   _____ nails were used.

   _____ nails are still in the box.

2. There are 11 checkers on a board. Eight of them are black. The rest are red. How many red checkers are on the board?

   _____ checkers are on a board.

   _____ checkers are black, and the rest are red.

   _____ red checkers are on the board.

3. Marty is ten years old. Her brother Larry is seven. Marty is how many years older than Larry?

   Marty's age is _____ years.

   Larry's age is _____ years.

   Marty is _____ years older than Larry.

4. Joye walked 11 blocks. Ann walked 2 blocks. Joye walked how much farther than Ann?

   Joye walked _____ blocks.

   Ann walked _____ blocks.

   Joye walked _____ blocks farther than Ann.

5. Twelve people are in a room. Five of them are men. How many are women?

   _____ women are in the room.

1.

2.

3.

4.   5.

Lesson 5
Addition and Subtraction Facts through 12

To check	5		To check	13	
$5 + 6 = 11$,	$+6$	These should	$13 - 4 = 9$,	-4	These should
subtract 6	$\overline{11}$	be the same.	add 4	$\overline{9}$	be the same.
from 11.	-6		to _____.	$+4$	
	$\overline{5}$			$\overline{13}$	

Add. Check each answer.

	a	b	c	d	e	f
1.	2 $+9$	8 $+4$	7 $+3$	3 $+8$	1 $+9$	6 $+6$
2.	9 $+3$	5 $+6$	4 $+8$	5 $+5$	7 $+4$	9 $+1$

Subtract. Check each answer.

	a	b	c	d	e	f
3.	1 0 -8	1 2 -7	1 1 -3	1 0 -4	1 1 -7	1 0 -7
4.	1 1 -9	1 2 -8	1 1 -8	1 2 -5	1 0 -6	1 0 -3

Lesson 5 Problem Solving

Answer each question.

1. Ben had some marbles. He gave two of them away and
   had nine left. How many marbles did he start with?

   Are you to add or subtract? _____

   How many marbles did he start with? _____

   1.

2. A full box has ten pieces of chalk. This box has only
   eight pieces. How many pieces are missing?

   Are you to add or subtract? _____

   How many pieces are missing? _____

   2.

3. Noah is 11 years old today. How old was he 4 years
   ago?

   Are you to add or subtract? _____

   How old was Noah 4 years ago? _____

   3.

4. Nine boys were playing ball. Then three more boys
   began to play. How many boys were playing ball then?

   Are you to add or subtract? _____

   How many boys were playing then? _____

   4.

5. Alyssa has as many sisters as brothers. She has
   five brothers. How many brothers and sisters does
   she have?

   Are you to add or subtract? _____

   How many brothers and
   sisters does Alyssa have? _____

   5.

6. Tricia invited 12 people to her party. Seven people
   came. How many people that were invited did not
   come?

   Are you to add or subtract? _____

   How many people did not come? _____

   6.

Lesson 6 Addition Facts through 18

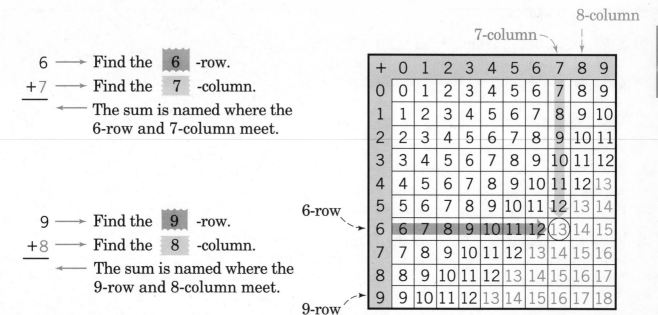

6 ⟶ Find the **6** -row.

+7 ⟶ Find the **7** -column.

⟵ The sum is named where the 6-row and 7-column meet.

9 ⟶ Find the **9** -row.

+8 ⟶ Find the **8** -column.

⟵ The sum is named where the 9-row and 8-column meet.

Add.

	a	b	c	d	e	f
1.	7 +6	8 +7	7 +4	9 +7	4 +9	8 +8
2.	5 +9	6 +4	6 +8	5 +8	8 +4	7 +8
3.	6 +9	5 +5	6 +7	9 +2	8 +6	4 +6
4.	5 +7	8 +9	9 +6	5 +6	9 +4	9 +9
5.	7 +9	8 +2	9 +8	8 +5	9 +1	4 +7
6.	9 +5	6 +6	2 +9	4 +8	7 +7	9 +3

Lesson 6   Problem Solving

Solve each problem.

1. Luciano worked nine hours on Monday. She worked seven hours on Tuesday. How many hours did she work in all on those two days?

    She worked _____ hours on Monday.

    She worked _____ hours on Tuesday.

    She worked _____ hours in all on those two days.

2. Alex has six windows to wash. Nadia has nine windows to wash. How many windows do they have to wash in all?

    Alex has _____ windows to wash.

    Nadia has _____ windows to wash.

    Together they have _____ windows to wash.

3. Seven cars are in the first row. Six cars are in the second row. How many cars are in the first two rows?

    _____ cars are in the first two rows.

4. There are nine men and eight women at work. How many people are at work?

    There are _____ people at work.

5. Andrew worked eight hours. Geraldo worked the same number of hours. How many hours did Andrew and Geraldo work in all?

    They worked _____ hours in all.

6. There are six plants in a box. Seven more plants are on a table. How many plants are there?

    There are _____ plants.

1.

2.

3.

4.

5.

6.

Lesson 7 Subtraction Facts through 18

6-column ~   8-column

$$13 \longrightarrow \text{Find 13 in}$$
$$\underline{-8} \longrightarrow \text{the } \boxed{8} \text{-column.}$$
$$\longleftarrow \text{The difference is named in the } \text{▨ at the end of that row.}$$

−	0	1	2	3	4	5	6	7	8	9
0	0	1	2	3	4	5	6	7	8	9
1	1	2	3	4	5	6	7	8	9	10
2	2	3	4	5	6	7	8	9	10	11
3	3	4	5	6	7	8	9	10	11	12
4	4	5	6	7	8	9	10	11	12	13
5	5	6	7	8	9	10	11	12	13	14
6	6	7	8	9	10	11	12	13	14	15
7	7	8	9	10	11	12	13	14	15	16
8	8	9	10	11	12	13	14	15	16	17
9	9	10	11	12	13	14	15	16	17	18

$$15 \longrightarrow \text{Find 15 in}$$
$$\underline{-6} \longrightarrow \text{the } \boxed{6} \text{-column.}$$
$$\longleftarrow \text{The difference is named in the } \text{▨ at the end of that row.}$$

CHAPTER 1

Subtract.

	a	b	c	d	e	f
1.	13 −5	14 −8	16 −7	10 −9	12 −5	14 −6
2.	17 −8	13 −7	12 −4	14 −5	15 −8	13 −6
3.	11 −7	18 −9	15 −6	11 −8	14 −7	13 −9
4.	16 −8	10 −5	12 −7	13 −4	12 −6	14 −9
5.	13 −8	12 −9	10 −1	15 −9	11 −3	10 −7
6.	15 −7	10 −3	17 −9	11 −6	16 −9	11 −4

Lesson 7   Problem Solving

Solve each problem.

1. Matt wants to collect 13 cars. He now has 5 cars.
   How many more cars does he need?

   Matt wants _____ cars.

   He now has _____ cars.

   He needs _____ more cars.

2. Susan bought 18 valentines. She mailed 9 of them.
   How many valentines does she have left?

   Susan bought _____ valentines.

   She mailed _____ of them.

   She has _____ valentines left.

3. Courtney had 16 stamps. She used some, and had
   7 left. How many stamps did she use?

   Courtney used _____ stamps.

4. Bret is 14 years old. Amy is 7. How many years
   older than Amy is Bret?

   Bret is _____ years older than Amy.

5. Fifteen bolts and nuts were on the table. Seven
   were bolts. How many were nuts?

   There were _____ nuts.

6. There are 17 machine parts in a drawer. Only 9
   are new parts. How many are not new parts?

   _____ parts are not new.

1.

2.

3.   **4.**

5.   **6.**

Lesson 8
Addition and Subtraction Facts through 18

| To check 6 + 8 = 14, subtract 8 from 14. | $\begin{array}{r} 6 \\ + 8 \\ \hline 14 \\ -8 \\ \hline 6 \end{array}$ | These should be the same. | To check 13 − 6 = 7, add _____ to 7. | $\begin{array}{r} 13 \\ -6 \\ \hline 7 \\ +6 \\ \hline 13 \end{array}$ | These should be the same. |

Add. Check each answer.

	a	b	c	d	e	f
1.	$\begin{array}{r} 5 \\ +9 \\ \hline \end{array}$	$\begin{array}{r} 9 \\ +7 \\ \hline \end{array}$	$\begin{array}{r} 6 \\ +6 \\ \hline \end{array}$	$\begin{array}{r} 7 \\ +4 \\ \hline \end{array}$	$\begin{array}{r} 9 \\ +8 \\ \hline \end{array}$	$\begin{array}{r} 3 \\ +7 \\ \hline \end{array}$
2.	$\begin{array}{r} 6 \\ +7 \\ \hline \end{array}$	$\begin{array}{r} 9 \\ +3 \\ \hline \end{array}$	$\begin{array}{r} 6 \\ +9 \\ \hline \end{array}$	$\begin{array}{r} 4 \\ +9 \\ \hline \end{array}$	$\begin{array}{r} 6 \\ +4 \\ \hline \end{array}$	$\begin{array}{r} 8 \\ +6 \\ \hline \end{array}$

Subtract. Check each answer.

3.	$\begin{array}{r} 1\,4 \\ -8 \\ \hline \end{array}$	$\begin{array}{r} 1\,8 \\ -9 \\ \hline \end{array}$	$\begin{array}{r} 1\,3 \\ -5 \\ \hline \end{array}$	$\begin{array}{r} 1\,5 \\ -6 \\ \hline \end{array}$	$\begin{array}{r} 1\,6 \\ -8 \\ \hline \end{array}$	$\begin{array}{r} 1\,2 \\ -7 \\ \hline \end{array}$
4.	$\begin{array}{r} 1\,3 \\ -6 \\ \hline \end{array}$	$\begin{array}{r} 1\,2 \\ -4 \\ \hline \end{array}$	$\begin{array}{r} 1\,3 \\ -4 \\ \hline \end{array}$	$\begin{array}{r} 1\,6 \\ -9 \\ \hline \end{array}$	$\begin{array}{r} 1\,5 \\ -7 \\ \hline \end{array}$	$\begin{array}{r} 1\,3 \\ -8 \\ \hline \end{array}$

Lesson 8 Problem Solving

Answer each problem.

1. Penny worked nine addition problems. She worked seven subtraction problems. How many problems did she work?

   Are you to add or subtract? _____

   How many problems
   did she work? _____

2. Six people were in the room. Then eight more people came in. How many people were in the room then?

   Are you to add or subtract? _____

   How many people were in the room then? _____

3. There were 18 chairs in a room. Nine of them were being used. How many were not being used?

   Are you to add or subtract? _____

   How many chairs
   were not being used? _____

4. Mr. Noe and Miss Leikel had 17 students absent. Mr. Noe had 9 absent. How many did Miss Leikel have absent?

   Are you to add or subtract? _____

   How many students were absent
   from Miss Leikel's class? _____

5. There were 14 children at the park. Five were boys. How many were girls?

   Are you to add or subtract? _____

   How many girls were at the park? _____

1.

2.

3.

4.

5.

CHAPTER 1 PRACTICE TEST
Addition and Subtraction (basic facts)

Add.

	a	b	c	d	e	f
1.	7 +8	4 +9	6 +5	2 +8	8 +6	7 +5
2.	9 +1	5 +8	8 +4	9 +2	8 +8	5 +9
3.	5 +7	6 +9	8 +3	8 +9	3 +8	9 +4
4.	9 +6	6 +7	9 +9	6 +6	7 +9	6 +4
5.	8 +5	3 +9	1 +9	7 +4	3 +7	6 +8

Subtract.

	a	b	c	d	e
6.	1 0 −6	1 4 −7	1 2 −3	1 5 −7	1 2 −8
7.	1 3 −4	1 6 −7	1 1 −9	1 0 −5	1 3 −6
8.	1 0 −2	1 4 −6	1 1 −6	1 2 −7	1 7 −9
9.	1 6 −8	1 1 −7	1 0 −3	1 4 −8	1 5 −8

CHAPTER 2 PRETEST
Numeration (0 through 10,000)

Write each number in expanded form.

a	b	c	d
1. 458	14	635	103
_____	_____	_____	_____

What digit is in the place named?

a	b
2. 463: ones	927: hundreds
_____ is in the ones place.	_____ is in the hundreds place.
3. 165: tens	94: ones
_____ is in the tens place.	_____ is in the ones place.

Compare each pair of numbers. Write < or >.

a	b	c	d
4. 0 ___ 8	3 ___ 13	61 ___ 51	37 ___ 35

Round each number to the place named.

a	b	c
5. 4,635: hundreds _____	742: tens _____	1,659: hundreds _____
6. 3,827: thousands _____	98: tens _____	485: hundreds _____

Solve each problem.

7. Name all of the even numbers between 12 and 20.   **7.**

_____   _____   _____

8. Name all of the odd numbers between 0 and 8.   **8.**

_____   _____   _____   _____

9. What is the largest number you can write using   **9.**
the digits 5, 6, and 2?

The largest number is _____.

10. What is the smallest number you can write using   **10.**
the digits 3, 8, and 6?

The smallest number is _____.

Lesson 1 Place Value

Use this chart to help you tell the value of each digit.

hundreds	tens	ones
3	6	2
The value of 3 is 3 hundreds or 300.	The value of 6 is 6 tens or 60.	The value of 2 is 2 ones or 2.

The expanded form of a number is the number written as a sum showing the place values.

The expanded form of 362 is 300 + 60 + 2.

Show the value of the 1 in each number.

	a	b	c	d
1.	214 __10__	105 _____	51 _____	18 _____

Name the value of the digit in the place named.

	a	b	c	d
2.	361: tens	105: ones	51: ones	18: tens
	__60__	_____	_____	_____
3.	471: hundreds	440: tens	276: tens	321: hundreds
	_____	_____	_____	_____

Write each number in expanded form.

	a	b	c	d
4.	492	45	329	560
	400 + 90 + 2	_____	_____	_____
5.	132	903	555	689
	_____	_____	_____	_____

Lesson 1 Problem Solving

Solve each problem.

1. Janna has cards arranged in three sets. One set has four rows each with 100 cards. The second set has three rows of ten cards. The third set has eight cards. Write the number of cards Janna has altogether.

   The four rows of 100 cards equal _____.

   The three rows of 10 cards equal _____.

   The number of cards is _____.

1.

2. Kenneth has eight hundred-dollar bills and three one-dollar bills. How much money does Kenneth have?

   The eight hundred-dollar bills equal _____.

   Since he has no _____ dollar bills, the tens place will have a _____.

   The three dollar bills equal _____.

   Kenneth has _____.

2.

3. Tameka is playing with a set of base-ten blocks. She can only find two hundreds blocks and five ones blocks. She has a lot of tens rows. How many tens rows should she use to show the largest number possible using two hundreds blocks and five ones blocks?

   She can use _____ tens rows to make _____.

3.

4. Ring the expanded form that does not express 876.

   800 + 70 + 6

   (500 + 300) + (10 + 60) + 6

   (300 + 500) + (60 + 60) + 6

4.

Lesson 2 Place Value

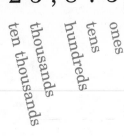

2 5 , 8 7 3

ten thousands
thousands
hundreds
tens
ones

In 3,472, which digit is in the hundreds place?

_____ is in the hundreds place.

Name the place of the underlined digit: 42,6<u>3</u>9

_____ is in the _____ place.

Which digit is in the place named?

a	b
1. 482: ones	3,119: hundreds
_____ is in the ones place.	_____ is in the hundreds place.
2. 673: tens	92: ones
_____ is in the tens place.	_____ is in the ones place.
3. 40,798: thousands	3,906: hundreds
_____ is in the thousands place.	_____ is in the hundreds place.
4. 974: ones	38,522: ten thousands
_____ is in the ones place.	_____ is in the ten thousands place.

Name the place of the underlined digit.

a	b
5. 64,7<u>9</u>3	1<u>7</u>,426
_____ is in the _____ place.	_____ is in the _____ place.
6. 45,<u>0</u>81	62<u>8</u>
_____ is in the _____ place.	_____ is in the _____ place.

Lesson 2 Problem Solving

Solve each problem.

1. Write the place value name for each digit in the number 81,637.

8 is in the _____ place.

1 is in the _____ place.

6 is in the _____ place.

3 is in the _____ place.

7 is in the _____ place.

2. Using the digits 3, 7, 0, and 1, write the greatest number possible.

The greatest place value used will be _____.

The smallest number will go in the _____ place.

The greatest number possible using the digits 3, 7, 0, and 1 is _____.

3. Write the number described:

2 is in the ones place.

The digit in the tens place is twice the digit in the ones place.

The digit in the hundreds place is two less than the digit in the ones place.

The digit in the thousands place is three times the digit in the ones place.

The digit in the ten thousands place is one half of the digit in the ones place.

_____ is in the ones place.

_____ is in the tens place.

_____ is in the hundreds place.

_____ is in the thousands place.

_____ is in the ten thousands place.

The number is _____.

1.

2.

3.

Lesson 3 Inequalities

Compare the numbers. Write < or >.
< means "is less than."
> means "is greater than."

Compare 21 and 45. Compare the value. Look at the tens. 2 tens is less than 4 tens. 21 is less than 45.

21 _<_ 45

Compare 358 and 321. Compare the value. Look at the hundreds. Since the digits in the hundreds place are the same, compare the tens. 5 tens is greater than 2 tens. 358 is greater than 321.

358 _>_ 321

Compare each pair of numbers. Write < or >.

	a	b	c	d
1.	0 ___ 4	4 ___ 8	5 ___ 10	3 ___ 1
2.	3 ___ 8	9 ___ 4	21 ___ 11	26 ___ 30
3.	47 ___ 59	29 ___ 93	23 ___ 423	489 ___ 389

Ring the greatest number.

	a	b	c	d
5.	6 3 13	9 13 3	8 7 1	22 14 26
6.	23 63 103	56 23 12	12 21 2	577 576 575

Solve each problem.

7. Andy lives 5 blocks from school. Karen lives 11 blocks from school. Jodie lives 1 block from school. Who lives the farthest from school?

_____ lives the farthest from school.

7.

8. Martin has 34 baseball cards in his collection. Samantha has 304 cards in her collection. Mr. Olsen has 3,400 cards in his collection. Who has the smallest collection?

_____ has the smallest baseball card collection.

8.

SPECTRUM MATHEMATICS
Red Book

Lesson 3
Inequalities

43

Lesson 4 Odd and Even Numbers

Even numbers end in 0, 2, 4, 6, or 8.

Here are some **even numbers:**

0, 2, 4, 6, 8, 10, 12, 14, 16, 18, 20

Odd numbers end in 1, 3, 5, 7, or 9.

Here are some **odd numbers:**

1, 3, 5, 7, 9, 11, 13, 15, 17, 19, 21

Ring all even numbers.

1. 3   7   2   4   6   8   21   0   10   81   13

Ring all odd numbers.

2. 25   58   44   76   21   45   78   42   35   60   13

Write the next greater even number.

a	b	c	d
3. 6 _____	2 _____	12 _____	30 _____
4. 34 _____	80 _____	56 _____	72 _____

Write the next smaller odd number.

a	b	c	d
5. 7 _____	3 _____	15 _____	91 _____
6. 77 _____	85 _____	33 _____	59 _____

Fill in the blanks with the type of numbers named.

7. even numbers; 4, _____, _____, _____, _____, 14, 16, 18

8. odd numbers; 11, _____, _____, _____, _____, 21, 23, 25

9. even numbers; _____, 2, _____, 6, _____, 10

10. The following children are sitting in a circle in the order named.   **10.**

Amy, Brian, Cody, Devin, Evan, Frannie, Gretta, Hank, Ingrid

They count off beginning with 1. All children with even numbers
will form Group E, and all children with odd numbers will form
Group O. Who will be in each group?

Group E has _____.

Group O has _____.

Lesson 5 Rounding

The steps for rounding are:

1) Find the digit in the place value to which you are rounding.

2) Look at the next digit to the right.

3) If that digit is 0, 1, 2, 3, or 4, do not change the first digit. The digits to the right change to zeros.

4) If that digit is 5, 6, 7, 8, or 9, add 1 to the first digit. The digits to the right change to zeros.

Round 3,478 to the nearest hundred.

4 is in the hundreds place.

Look at the 7.

Increase 4 to 5.

3,478 to the nearest hundred is 3,500.

Round 912 to the nearest ten.

1 is in the tens place.

Look at the 2.

Do not change the 1.

912 to the nearest ten is 910.

Round each number to the nearest ten.

	a	b	c	d
1.	547 _____	1,059 _____	36 _____	124 _____
2.	65,014 _____	5,988 _____	13 _____	941 _____

Round each number to the nearest thousand.

	a	b	c	d
3.	1,257 _____	8,050 _____	936 _____	7,124 _____
4.	56,134 _____	91,188 _____	13,884 _____	2,941 _____

Round each number to the place named.

	a	b	c
5.	166: tens _____	11,456: hundreds _____	4,153: hundreds _____
6.	845: tens _____	5,698: thousands _____	298: hundreds _____
7.	42: tens _____	28,409: ten thousands _____	783: tens _____
8.	78: hundreds _____	8,794: thousands _____	384: hundreds _____

Lesson 5 Problem Solving

Solve each problem.

1. Ms. Macinlini makes $56,897 a year as a bank manager. She is filling out a credit application and needs to write in an estimated income. What amount will she use if she rounds to the nearest thousands?

   Which digit is in the thousands place? _____

   Which digit do you look at to decide how to round ____?

   The rounded estimated income is _____.

2. The Fouts are buying a new house that has 2,355 square feet. How many square feet is this rounded to the nearest hundred?

   Which digit is in the hundreds place? _____

   Which digit will be in the hundreds place of the rounded number? _____

   The square footage to the nearest hundred is _____.

3. The Jewel warehouse stores paperback books for the corner bookstore. At last count, they had 2,617 books stored. To the nearest hundred, how many books are stored in the warehouse?

   There are about _____ books stored.

4. Jon collects postcards. At the end of one year, he has 362 postcards. To the nearest ten, how many postcards does Jon have?

   Jon has about _____ postcards.

5. Cecil's ant farm contains 39,949 ants. To the nearest thousand, how many ants does Cecil have?

   There are about _____ ants in the farm.

1.

2.

3.

4.

5.

CHAPTER 2 PRACTICE TEST
Numeration (0 through 10,000)

Write each number in expanded form.

	a	b	c	d
1.	287	24	649	808
	_____	_____	_____	_____

Which digit is in the place named?

a

b

2. 978: ones

_____ is in the ones place.

1,463: hundreds

_____ is in the hundreds place.

3. 897: tens

_____ is in the tens place.

2,135: hundreds

_____ is in the hundreds place.

Compare each pair of numbers. Write < or >.

	a	b	c	d
4.	10 ___ 24	4 ___ 1	52 ___ 10	3 ___ 17
5.	5 ___ 8	11 ___ 4	28 ___ 21	76 ___ 77

Ring the even numbers.

6. 6   8   2   15   36   82   23   40   0   29   11   456

Ring the odd numbers.

7. 18   35   28   49   64   13   4   6   8   16   9   149

Round each number to the place named.

a

b

c

8. 3,645: hundreds _____   119: tens _____   1,315: hundreds _____

9. 1,958: thousands _____   46: tens _____   656: hundreds _____

Solve the problem.

10. What is the greatest number you can write using the digits 4, 9, 0, and 6?

10.

The greatest number is _____.

CHAPTER 3 PRETEST
Addition and Subtraction (2-digit; no renaming)

Add.

	a	*b*	*c*	*d*	*e*	*f*
1.	3 +6	4 3 +6	1 +4	5 1 +4	2 +5	8 2 +5
2.	5 7 +2	2 6 +1	4 4 +3	2 3 +4	4 2 +3	2 1 +5
3.	4 +3 1	5 +4 3	4 +6 2	3 +4 3	5 +1 2	7 +2 0
4.	5 4 +3 1	2 6 +1 2	4 5 +3 3	6 7 +2 1	4 2 +3 3	2 2 +1 3
5.	3 2 +3 1	2 4 +2 4	3 6 +6 1	2 0 +1 9	4 5 +2 3	3 2 +2 1

Subtract.

	a	*b*	*c*	*d*	*e*	*f*
6.	7 −4	3 7 − 4	5 −2	4 5 −2	8 −6	3 8 −6
7.	3 8 −4	2 7 −6	5 4 −3	2 9 −7	6 8 −2	2 6 − 3
8.	5 4 −2 3	6 9 −2 4	3 7 −2 1	8 8 −2 4	9 3 −2 1	8 7 −3 7
9.	2 8 −1 3	5 4 −3 4	8 7 −2 6	5 4 −2 1	5 0 −4 0	3 7 −1 0

CHAPTER 3

Lesson 1   Addition (1- and 2-digit)

Add the ones.	Add the tens.		Add the ones.	Add the tens.

```
  3 6        3 6        3 6              6          6          6
+   2      +   2      +   2          + 4 1      + 4 1      + 4 1
             ___        ___                       ___        ___
              8         3 8                         7        4 7
```

Add.

	a	b	c	d	e	f
1.	3 +5	2 3 + 5	2 +3	4 2 + 3	5 +1	2 5 + 1
2.	3 +4	3 +6 4	4 +5	4 +5 5	2 +5	2 +8 5
3.	2 +4	1 2 +4	2 2 +4	3 2 +4	4 2 +4	5 2 +4
4.	5 +6 3	6 +3 1	2 4 +3	9 2 +2	5 7 +1	2 +4 1
5.	4 1 +3	2 1 +2	3 +6 3	2 +8 4	2 1 +6	4 +1 4
6.	8 +5 1	6 2 +4	2 5 +3	6 +3 3	2 +5 1	5 +4 3
7.	3 6 +2	4 2 +5	2 +5 1	6 0 +8	5 +2 1	3 4 +2

Lesson 1 Problem Solving

Solve each problem.

1. John has 32 red marbles and 5 green marbles. How many red and green marbles does he have?

   John has _____ red and green marbles.

   1.

2. Su-Lee had 5 paper cups. She bought 24 more. Now how many paper cups does she have?

   She has _____ paper cups.

   2.

3. On the way to work, Michael counted 41 cars and 7 trucks. How many cars and trucks did he count?

   Michael counted _____ cars and trucks.

   3.

4. Mark worked all the problems on a test. He had 24 right answers and 4 wrong ones. How many problems were on the test?

   There were _____ problems on the test.

   4.

5. Shea works with 12 women and 6 men. How many people does she work with?

   Shea works with _____ people.

   5.

6. Four men and 11 women are on the bus. How many people are on the bus?

   _____ people are on the bus.

   6.

7. Marta weighs 20 kilograms. Her baby brother weighs 4 kilograms. How much do they weigh together?

   They weigh _____ kilograms together.

   7.

Lesson 2 Addition (2-digit)

Add the ones. Add the tens.

```
   36        36        36
  +43       +43       +43
            ———       ———
             9        79
```

```
   25
  +61
  ———
   86
```
↑↑ ——— Add the ones.
└——— Add the tens.

Add.

	a	b	c	d	e	f
1.	2 3 +4 5	6 3 +2 1	4 5 +2 2	6 1 +3 0	4 2 +3 5	6 0 +2 5
2.	4 8 +4 1	5 2 +1 4	3 2 +5 4	6 3 +2 0	2 1 +3 8	4 5 +5 2
3.	3 4 +2 2	4 1 +2 5	3 6 +2 2	5 1 +4 0	8 3 +1 2	4 2 +3 0
4.	6 3 +2 4	3 0 +5 8	2 7 +1 2	4 4 +2 3	6 2 +1 4	3 5 +5 3
5.	2 4 +3 1	5 2 +3 2	4 2 +2 7	5 1 +3 3	1 6 +2 0	4 3 +2 3
6.	3 4 +2 5	6 4 +2 3	1 8 +4 1	5 4 +2 4	4 1 +2 7	1 4 +3 2

Lesson 2 Problem Solving

Solve each problem.

1. There are 12 boys and 13 girls in Jean's class. How many students are in her class?

   There are _____ students in her class.

2. Emily scored 32 baskets. She missed 23 times. How many times did she try to score?

   Emily tried to score _____ times.

3. One store ordered 52 bicycles. Another store ordered 45 bicycles. How many bicycles did both stores order?

   Both stores ordered _____ bicycles.

4. One bear cub weighs 64 kilograms. Another bear cub is 22 kilograms heavier. How much does the heavier cub weigh?

   The heavier cub weighs_____ kilograms.

5. Joshua rode the bus 42 blocks east and 25 blocks south. How many blocks did Joshua ride the bus?

   Joshua rode the bus _____ blocks.

6. Forty-three women and 35 men came to the meeting. How many people came to the meeting?

   _____ people came to the meeting.

7. Sixty-eight seats were filled, and 21 were empty. How many seats were there?

   There were _____ seats.

1.	
2.	**3.**
4.	**5.**
6.	**7.**

Lesson 3 Subtraction (1- and 2-digit)

	Subtract the ones.	Subtract the tens.			Subtract the ones.	Subtract the tens.
47 -2	47 -2 5	47 -2 45	64 -23	64 -23 1	64 -23 41

CHAPTER 3

Subtract.

	a	*b*	*c*	*d*	*e*	*f*
1.	9 -3	4 9 $-\ 3$	5 -2	3 5 $-\ 2$	7 -1	8 7 $-\ 1$
2.	8 -2	7 8 $-\ 2$	4 -3	6 4 $-\ 3$	9 -9	8 9 $-\ 9$
3.	4 5 $-\ 3$	3 6 $-\ 4$	7 8 $-\ 5$	4 2 $-\ 2$	3 8 $-\ 8$	6 5 $-\ 4$
4.	4 9 $-2\ 6$	3 7 $-1\ 6$	5 8 $-2\ 3$	4 9 $-3\ 1$	7 8 $-4\ 5$	7 3 $-2\ 0$
5.	5 8 $-2\ 7$	6 9 $-3\ 1$	4 2 $-2\ 1$	4 9 $-1\ 9$	8 4 $-2\ 3$	7 8 $-6\ 4$
6.	7 8 $-2\ 1$	6 7 $-3\ 1$	4 0 $-2\ 0$	5 6 $-3\ 6$	4 5 $-2\ 3$	9 2 $-2\ 1$
7.	5 6 $-4\ 1$	8 5 $-6\ 3$	9 4 $-3\ 2$	7 7 $-4\ 6$	9 9 $-3\ 2$	8 6 $-2\ 3$

Lesson 3 Problem Solving

Solve each problem.

1. Beth worked 27 problems. She got 6 wrong answers. How many answers did she get right?

    Beth got _____ answers right.

2. There were 96 parts in a box. Four parts were broken. How many parts were not broken?

    _____ parts were not broken.

3. At noon the temperature was 28 degrees Celsius. At nine o'clock in the evening, it was 14 degrees Celsius. How many degrees Celsius did the temperature drop?

    It dropped _____ degrees Celsius.

4. Clark had 75 cents. He spent 25 cents for some paper. How much money did he have left?

    Clark had _____ cents left.

5. There are 72 houses in Kyle's neighborhood. Kyle delivers papers to all but 21 of them. How many houses does he deliver papers to?

    He delivers papers to _____ houses.

6. Ninety-five students were in the gym. Thirty-four were boys. How many were girls?

    _____ students were girls.

7. A rope is 47 inches long. A wire is 17 inches long. How much longer is the rope?

    The rope is _____ inches longer.

1.	
2.	**3.**
4.	**5.**
6.	**7.**

Lesson 4 Subtraction (2-digit)

To check
37 − 24 = 13,
add 24
to _____ .

$$\begin{array}{r} 37 \\ -24 \\ \hline 13 \\ +24 \\ \hline 37 \end{array}$$

These should be the same.

To check
59 − 29 = 30,

add _____
to 30.

$$\begin{array}{r} 59 \\ -29 \\ \hline 30 \\ +29 \\ \hline 59 \end{array}$$

These should be the same.

Subtract. Check each answer.

	a	b	c	d	e	f
1.	59 −34	27 −14	85 −23	78 −23	47 −24	59 −26
2.	85 −25	48 −32	56 −24	96 −35	40 −30	92 −81
3.	74 −23	58 −26	75 −24	38 −23	45 −35	88 −35
4.	67 −24	87 −24	59 −36	58 −24	79 −54	84 −23

Lesson 4 Problem Solving

Solve each problem.

1. Mr. Ming wants to build a fence 58 meters long. He has 27 meters of fence completed. How much of the fence is left to build?

   _____ meters of fence is left to build.

2. Mrs. Boyle is taking an 89-mile trip. She has traveled 64 miles. How much farther must she travel?

   Mrs. Boyle must travel _____ more miles.

3. Sean had 95 cents. Then he spent 45 cents. How many cents did he have left?

   Sean had _____ cents left.

4. Kevin scored 62 points and Bianca scored 78 points. How many more points did Bianca score than Kevin?

   Bianca scored _____ more points.

5. Darien lives 38 blocks from the ballpark. Kelly lives 25 blocks from the ballpark. How much farther away from the ballpark does Darien live than Kelly?

   Darien lives _____ blocks farther away.

6. Eighty-four students were in the pool. Fifty of them were boys. How many girls were in the pool?

   _____ girls were in the pool.

7. Chad said that 88 buses stop at Division Street each day. So far, 13 buses have stopped. How many more buses should stop today?

   _____ more buses should stop.

1.	
2.	**3.**
4.	**5.**
6.	**7.**

Lesson 5 Addition and Subtraction Review

To check   43
43 + 14 = 57,   + 14
subtract 14   57   These should
from _____.   − 14   be the same.
                          43

To check   57
57 − 14 = 43,   − 14
                           43   These should
add _____   + 14   be the same.
to 43.   57

Add. Check each answer.

	a	b	c	d	e	f
1.	2 7 +3 1	4 2 +5 1	2 6 +3 0	1 4 +5 2	2 3 +7 2	6 5 +2 2
2.	4 4 +2 4	3 1 +2 7	6 4 +1 4	3 2 +2 0	4 2 +3 6	4 6 +2 3

Subtract. Check each answer.

3.	7 8 −2 3	4 8 −1 3	2 7 −1 6	5 8 −2 6	6 7 −2 4	3 8 −1 6
4.	7 5 −6 1	4 6 −2 6	3 9 −1 0	4 5 −2 3	6 7 −4 1	3 8 −1 5

Lesson 5 Problem Solving

Solve each problem.

1. Mrs. Dial weighs 55 kilograms. Her son weighs 32 kilograms. How much more than her son does Mrs. Dial weigh?

   She weighs _____ kilograms more.

2. Mitzi planted 55 flower seeds. Only 23 of them grew. How many did not grow?

   _____ seeds did not grow.

3. Springfield has 48 mail trucks. Twelve are not being used today. How many mail trucks are being used?

   _____ mail trucks are being used.

4. A mail carrier delivered 38 letters and picked up 15. How many more letters were delivered than were picked up?

   The carrier delivered _____ more letters.

5. A city has 89 mail carriers. One day 77 carriers were at work. How many were not at work?

   _____ carriers were not at work.

6. Our mail carrier walks about 32 miles each week. About how many miles does our carrier walk in two weeks?

   Our mail carrier walks about _____ miles in two weeks.

7. Ms. Tottle worked at a store for 23 years. She then worked 26 years at a bank. How many years did she work at these two places?

   She worked _____ years at these two places.

1.	
2.	3.
4.	5.
6.	7.

CHAPTER 3 PRACTICE TEST
Addition and Subtraction (2-digit; no renaming)

Add or subtract. Check each answer.

	a	*b*	*c*	*d*	*e*	*f*
1.	4 +2	2 4 +2	3 6 +3	4 +2 1	7 2 +4	9 +3 0
2.	3 6 +2 1	4 1 +3 8	6 5 +2 2	4 1 +2 6	3 5 +5 0	6 6 +2 1
3.	7 −2	3 7 −2	4 5 −4	2 6 −3	4 9 −8	2 7 −5
4.	4 8 −2 3	6 5 −2 4	4 5 −2 2	6 8 −2 8	5 4 −2 2	6 7 −3 0

Solve.

5. Miss Jones has 32 students. Mr. Lum has 26 students.
How many students are in the two classes?

There are _____ students in the two classes.

CHAPTER 3

CHAPTER 4 PRETEST
Addition and Subtraction (2-digit; with renaming)

Add.

	a	*b*	*c*	*d*	*e*	*f*
1.	53 +6	24 +2	2 +35	8 +81	64 +3	25 +2
2.	36 +5	54 +8	8 +39	2 +59	48 +8	26 +7
3.	42 +33	72 +14	54 +23	61 +28	19 +40	26 +52
4.	54 +27	35 +36	59 +38	54 +19	27 +48	39 +39
5.	49 +23	62 +17	43 +21	48 +48	26 +40	56 +37

Subtract.

	a	*b*	*c*	*d*	*e*	*f*
6.	37 −3	29 −4	54 −4	87 −2	56 −5	89 −6
7.	47 −9	72 −5	45 −7	55 −9	40 −5	34 −7
8.	54 −12	42 −30	75 −64	46 −23	93 −81	89 −41
9.	73 −25	85 −49	92 −24	64 −56	77 −48	88 −38

CHAPTER 4

Lesson 1 Addition (1- and 2-digit)

Add the ones.
Rename 13 as 10 + 3.

Add the tens.

$$
\begin{array}{r} 54 \\ +9 \\ \hline \end{array}
\qquad
\begin{array}{r} 4 \\ +9 \\ \hline 13 \end{array} \text{ or } 10 + 3
\qquad
\begin{array}{r} ^{1}54 \\ +9 \\ \hline 3 \end{array}
\qquad
\begin{array}{r} ^{1}54 \\ +9 \\ \hline 63 \end{array}
$$

Add.

	a	b	c	d	e	f
1.	27 +5	35 +8	87 +4	38 +9	42 +8	46 +5
2.	45 +9	27 +7	7 +38	20 +65	24 +9	8 +38
3.	27 +3	45 +6	8 +36	9 +29	6 +58	42 +9
4.	76 +7	3 +47	4 +26	27 +4	5 +18	9 +19
5.	6 +15	41 +9	52 +8	65 +9	7 +38	6 +16
6.	9 +28	36 +7	59 +2	7 +36	4 +47	9 +38
7.	46 +8	9 +25	8 +68	4 +59	85 +5	78 +7

Lesson 1   Problem Solving

Solve each problem.

1. Last year there were 44 monkeys on an island. There are 8 more monkeys this year. How many monkeys are on the island now?

   There were _____ monkeys last year.

   There are _____ more monkeys this year.

   There are _____ monkeys on the island now.

   1.

2. There were 72 children and 9 adults in our group at the zoo. How many people were in our group?

   _____ children were in our group.

   _____ adults were in our group.

   _____ people were in our group.

   2.

3. One group of monkeys was fed 6 kilograms of fruit. Another group was fed 19 kilograms. How much fruit was that in all?

   That was _____ kilograms of fruit in all.

   3.

4. The children drank 68 cartons of milk. There were 8 full cartons left. How many cartons of milk were there to start with?

   There were _____ cartons of milk to start with.

   4.

5. A zoo has 87 kinds of snakes. They are getting 4 new kinds. How many kinds will they have then?

   They will have _____ kinds of snakes.

   5.

Lesson 2   Addition (2-digit)

Add the ones.
Rename 15 as 10 + 5.

Add the tens.

$$\begin{array}{r} 48 \\ +27 \\ \hline \end{array}$$

$$\begin{array}{r} 8 \\ +7 \\ \hline 15 \text{ or } 10 + 5 \end{array}$$

$$\begin{array}{r} 1 \\ 48 \\ +27 \\ \hline 5 \end{array}$$

$$\begin{array}{r} 1 \\ 48 \\ +27 \\ \hline 75 \end{array}$$

Add.

	a	b	c	d	e	f
1.	37 +25	48 +37	26 +54	35 +29	54 +18	62 +29
2.	29 +28	38 +37	47 +25	63 +27	79 +19	64 +17
3.	58 +26	45 +18	27 +57	44 +29	36 +36	77 +17
4.	49 +48	26 +37	73 +19	18 +28	15 +47	29 +27
5.	18 +55	28 +24	38 +37	48 +43	58 +16	68 +28
6.	26 +66	19 +54	57 +29	45 +36	52 +18	33 +29
7.	35 +56	47 +28	31 +39	29 +59	67 +16	55 +28

Lesson 2 Problem Solving

Solve each problem.

1. January has 31 days. February has 29 days this year. How many days are in the two months?

    There are _____ days in January.

    There are _____ days in February this year.

    There are _____ days in January and February.

2. Jeff weighs 46 kilograms. His father is 36 kilograms heavier. How much does Jeff's father weigh?

    Jeff weighs _____ kilograms.

    His father is _____ kilograms heavier.

    His father weighs _____ kilograms.

3. Lauren had 29 points. She earned 13 more. How many points did she have then?

    Lauren had _____ points.

    She earned _____ more.

    She had _____ points then.

4. Adam gained 18 pounds in the last year. A year ago he weighed 59 pounds. How much does he weigh today?

    Adam weighs _____ pounds today.

5. Kathy read 25 pages of a story. She has 36 more pages to read. How many pages are in the story?

    There are _____ pages in the story.

1.
2.
3.

4.	5.

Lesson 3 Subtraction (1-digit)

	To subtract the ones, rename 63 as "5 tens and 13 ones."	Subtract the ones.	Subtract the tens.

$$\begin{array}{r} 63 \\ -9 \\ \hline \end{array}$$

$$\begin{array}{r} {}^{5}6\,{}^{13}\!\!\not3 \\ -9 \\ \hline \end{array}$$

$$\begin{array}{r} {}^{5}6\,{}^{13}\!\!\not3 \\ -9 \\ \hline 4 \end{array}$$

$$\begin{array}{r} {}^{5}6\,{}^{13}\!\!\not3 \\ -9 \\ \hline 54 \end{array}$$

CHAPTER 4

Subtract.

	a	b	c	d	e	f
1.	5 3 −8	2 7 −9	4 6 −9	5 4 −5	3 2 −6	6 5 −7
2.	2 8 −9	4 8 −9	3 5 −6	4 4 −7	6 7 −8	9 2 −9
3.	5 2 −6	6 2 −4	6 1 −6	7 3 −5	5 0 −9	4 2 −5
4.	9 6 −8	7 3 −6	8 0 −7	4 2 −3	6 3 −4	5 1 −9
5.	9 4 −8	8 8 −9	3 3 −4	2 7 −9	4 6 −8	6 4 −7
6.	2 3 −9	7 6 −8	4 0 −4	4 1 −6	5 3 −7	2 5 −7
7.	4 7 −8	3 1 −7	8 2 −8	7 4 −6	9 3 −9	6 0 −5

Lesson 3   Problem Solving

Solve each problem.

1. There were 48 words on a spelling test. Sarah missed 9 of them. How many words did she spell correctly?

   There were _____ words on the test.

   Sarah missed _____ words.

   She spelled _____ words correctly.

2. Ryan earned 91 points. Mike earned 5 points less than Ryan. How many points did Mike earn?

   Ryan earned _____ points.

   Mike earned _____ points less than Ryan.

   Mike earned _____ points.

3. Sheila lost 7 of the 45 games she played. How many games did she win?

   She won _____ games.

4. Travis had 50 tickets to sell. He sold some and had 6 left. How many tickets did he sell?

   Travis sold _____ tickets.

5. There were 73 books in the classroom library. Some of the books are checked out. Seven are still there. How many books are checked out?

   _____ books are checked out.

6. Angela's great-grandfather is 82 years old. How old was he 4 years ago?

   Four years ago he was_____ years old.

1.

2.

3.

4.

5.

6.

Lesson 4 Subtraction (2-digit)

To subtract the ones,
rename 92 as "8 tens
and 12 ones."

Subtract
the ones.

Subtract
the tens.

```
            8 12          8 12          8 12
  92         9 2          9 2          9 2
-38        -3 8         -3 8         -3 8
                                4            54
```

CHAPTER 4

Subtract.

	a	b	c	d	e	f
1.	35 −17	27 −19	54 −37	63 −26	84 −59	28 −19
2.	42 −24	56 −39	41 −27	53 −15	86 −78	92 −26
3.	43 −15	37 −29	26 −19	55 −36	43 −27	28 −19
4.	54 −26	35 −18	22 −15	56 −29	38 −19	31 −18
5.	83 −25	94 −16	65 −39	73 −17	80 −28	92 −35
6.	35 −26	90 −55	56 −27	41 −16	50 −38	61 −15
7.	52 −18	75 −38	47 −39	60 −11	86 −59	94 −48

Lesson 4 Problem Solving

Solve each problem.

1. Joseph weighs 95 pounds. Zach weighs 26 pounds less than Joseph. How much does Zach weigh?

   Joseph weighs _____ pounds.

   Zach weighs _____ pounds less than Joseph.

   Zach weighs _____ pounds.

2. There are 73 children in the gym. Forty-five of them are boys. How many girls are in the gym?

   There are _____ children in the gym.

   There are _____ boys in the gym.

   There are _____ girls in the gym.

3. A store has 84 bicycles. They have 45 girls' bicycles. How many boys' bicycles do they have?

   _____ bicycles are boys' bicycles.

4. It takes 50 points to win a prize. Paige has 38 points. How many more points does Paige need to win a prize?

   Paige needs _____ points.

5. Allison has 19 more pages to read in a book. The book has 46 pages in all. How many pages has Allison already read?

   Allison has already read _____ pages.

6. The Tigers scored 33 points. The Bears scored 18 points. How many more points did the Tigers score than the Bears?

   The Tigers scored _____ more points.

1.

2.

3.

4.

5.

6.

Lesson 5 Addition and Subtraction Review

To check	34		To check	53	
34 + 19 = 53,	+19	These should be the same.	53 − 19 = 34,	−19	These should be the same.
subtract 19	53		add _____	34	
from _____ .	−19		to 34.	+19	
	34			53	

Add. Check each answer.

	a	b	c	d	e	f
1.	5 4 +7	4 6 +9	6 3 +1 8	5 8 +2 7	2 1 +4 9	4 5 +4 6
2.	2 6 +3 8	3 7 +1 9	4 1 +9	5 8 +1 8	6 7 +2 7	3 5 +3 8

Subtract. Check each answer.

3.	6 2 −8	4 8 −9	3 5 −1 6	9 6 −2 9	5 2 −1 4	4 3 −5
4.	3 6 −1 8	5 7 −8	6 7 −1 9	5 2 −1 7	5 1 −2 3	6 0 −4 6

Lesson 5　Problem Solving

Answer each question.

1. This morning the temperature was 75 degrees. This afternoon it was 83 degrees. How many degrees did it go up?

   Are you to add
   or subtract? _____

   How many degrees did
   the temperature go up? _____

1.

2. There were 45 people at a meeting. After 28 of them left, how many people were still at the meeting?

   Are you to add
   or subtract? _____

   How many people
   were still at the meeting? _____

2.

3. Renée drove 67 miles in the morning and 24 miles in the afternoon. How far did she drive?

   Are you to add
   or subtract? _____

   How far did she drive? _____

3.

4. Christopher is 54 inches tall. His sister is 36 inches tall. How much taller is Christopher?

   Are you to add
   or subtract? _____

   How much taller is
   Christopher than his sister? _____

4.

5. A clown has 26 orange balloons and 28 blue balloons. How many balloons is that?

   Are you to add
   or subtract? _____

   How many orange and
   blue balloons are there? _____

5.

CHAPTER 4 PRACTICE TEST
Addition and Subtraction (2-digit; with renaming)

Add. Check each answer.

	a	b	c	d	e	f
1.	3 6 +7	4 5 +9	8 +2 3	1 7 +7	8 +4 4	5 8 +6
2.	1 7 +2 5	2 6 +4 8	4 3 +3 8	7 4 +1 9	7 8 +1 8	6 5 +1 6

Subtract. Check each answer.

3.	2 6 −8	5 4 −9	6 1 −3	2 7 −9	5 4 −6	6 6 −9
4.	3 6 −1 7	7 2 −4 4	3 8 −1 9	7 4 −2 6	9 3 −8 9	8 2 −5 7

Solve.

5. Fifty-four girls and 27 boys came to the meeting.

How many boys and girls came to the meeting?

_____ boys and girls came to the meeting.

CHAPTER 5 PRETEST
Addition and Subtraction (2- and 3-digit; with renaming)

Add.

	a	*b*	*c*	*d*	*e*	*f*
1.	5 +6	5 0 +6 0	7 +8	7 0 +8 0	9 0 +8 0	7 0 +7 0
2.	5 3 +9 5	4 4 +7 4	8 2 +9 6	6 7 +7 0	5 5 +5 2	7 3 +8 6
3.	6 3 +7 8	8 2 +8 9	9 7 +2 7	5 6 +7 5	8 8 +8 8	9 7 +4 4
4.	2 6 +5 3	6 6 +2 5	7 4 +6 5	3 9 +8 7	8 2 +1 7	7 6 +7 2
5.	5 9 +5 9	7 3 +1 5	8 3 +6 7	5 4 +7 2	6 3 +7 0	3 5 +4 5

Subtract.

	a	*b*	*c*	*d*	*e*	*f*
6.	1 6 −7	1 6 0 −7 0	1 5 −9	1 5 0 −9 0	1 4 0 −6 0	1 7 0 −8 0
7.	1 3 6 −5 3	1 6 5 −7 4	1 5 4 −9 0	1 8 6 −9 3	1 7 9 −8 2	1 4 7 −6 7
8.	1 4 6 −9 7	1 5 8 −6 9	1 7 2 −8 5	1 6 3 −7 7	1 2 5 −5 8	1 1 6 −3 9
9.	1 7 6 −5 3	1 8 4 −3 5	1 5 4 −7 2	1 5 3 −7 4	1 4 6 −3 2	1 0 7 −4 0

Lesson 1 Addition and Subtraction (tens)

$$\begin{array}{r} 8 \\ +6 \\ \hline 14 \end{array} \qquad \begin{array}{r} 8 \\ +6 \\ \hline \end{array} \qquad \begin{array}{r} 80 \\ +60 \\ \hline \end{array} \qquad \begin{array}{r} 80 \\ +60 \\ \hline 140 \end{array} \qquad \bigg| \qquad \begin{array}{r} 14 \\ -6 \\ \hline \end{array} \qquad \begin{array}{r} 14 \\ -6 \\ \hline 8 \end{array} \qquad \begin{array}{r} 140 \\ -60 \\ \hline \end{array} \qquad \begin{array}{r} 140 \\ -60 \\ \hline 80 \end{array}$$

If $8 + 6 = 14$, then $80 + 60 =$ _____. | If $14 - 6 = 8$, then $140 - 60 =$ _____.

Add.

	a	b	c	d	e	f
1.	$\begin{array}{r} 7 \\ +8 \\ \hline \end{array}$	$\begin{array}{r} 70 \\ +80 \\ \hline \end{array}$	$\begin{array}{r} 6 \\ +9 \\ \hline \end{array}$	$\begin{array}{r} 60 \\ +90 \\ \hline \end{array}$	$\begin{array}{r} 3 \\ +8 \\ \hline \end{array}$	$\begin{array}{r} 30 \\ +80 \\ \hline \end{array}$
2.	$\begin{array}{r} 7 \\ +5 \\ \hline \end{array}$	$\begin{array}{r} 70 \\ +50 \\ \hline \end{array}$	$\begin{array}{r} 8 \\ +9 \\ \hline \end{array}$	$\begin{array}{r} 80 \\ +90 \\ \hline \end{array}$	$\begin{array}{r} 4 \\ +6 \\ \hline \end{array}$	$\begin{array}{r} 40 \\ +60 \\ \hline \end{array}$
3.	$\begin{array}{r} 70 \\ +40 \\ \hline \end{array}$	$\begin{array}{r} 50 \\ +90 \\ \hline \end{array}$	$\begin{array}{r} 30 \\ +90 \\ \hline \end{array}$	$\begin{array}{r} 70 \\ +70 \\ \hline \end{array}$	$\begin{array}{r} 90 \\ +40 \\ \hline \end{array}$	$\begin{array}{r} 80 \\ +40 \\ \hline \end{array}$
4.	$\begin{array}{r} 20 \\ +90 \\ \hline \end{array}$	$\begin{array}{r} 60 \\ +60 \\ \hline \end{array}$	$\begin{array}{r} 70 \\ +60 \\ \hline \end{array}$	$\begin{array}{r} 90 \\ +10 \\ \hline \end{array}$	$\begin{array}{r} 70 \\ +90 \\ \hline \end{array}$	$\begin{array}{r} 80 \\ +80 \\ \hline \end{array}$

Subtract.

	a	b	c	d	e	f
5.	$\begin{array}{r} 13 \\ -5 \\ \hline \end{array}$	$\begin{array}{r} 130 \\ -50 \\ \hline \end{array}$	$\begin{array}{r} 17 \\ -8 \\ \hline \end{array}$	$\begin{array}{r} 170 \\ -80 \\ \hline \end{array}$	$\begin{array}{r} 12 \\ -6 \\ \hline \end{array}$	$\begin{array}{r} 120 \\ -60 \\ \hline \end{array}$
6.	$\begin{array}{r} 15 \\ -6 \\ \hline \end{array}$	$\begin{array}{r} 150 \\ -60 \\ \hline \end{array}$	$\begin{array}{r} 14 \\ -5 \\ \hline \end{array}$	$\begin{array}{r} 140 \\ -50 \\ \hline \end{array}$	$\begin{array}{r} 18 \\ -9 \\ \hline \end{array}$	$\begin{array}{r} 180 \\ -90 \\ \hline \end{array}$
7.	$\begin{array}{r} 140 \\ -80 \\ \hline \end{array}$	$\begin{array}{r} 110 \\ -70 \\ \hline \end{array}$	$\begin{array}{r} 160 \\ -80 \\ \hline \end{array}$	$\begin{array}{r} 130 \\ -60 \\ \hline \end{array}$	$\begin{array}{r} 170 \\ -90 \\ \hline \end{array}$	$\begin{array}{r} 120 \\ -50 \\ \hline \end{array}$
8.	$\begin{array}{r} 130 \\ -90 \\ \hline \end{array}$	$\begin{array}{r} 160 \\ -70 \\ \hline \end{array}$	$\begin{array}{r} 150 \\ -80 \\ \hline \end{array}$	$\begin{array}{r} 120 \\ -80 \\ \hline \end{array}$	$\begin{array}{r} 140 \\ -90 \\ \hline \end{array}$	$\begin{array}{r} 110 \\ -40 \\ \hline \end{array}$

Lesson 1 Problem Solving

Answer each question.

1. Nicholas is on a trip of 170 kilometers. So far he has gone 90 kilometers. How many more kilometers must he go?

   Are you to add or subtract? _____

   How many more kilometers must he go? _____

   1.

2. A school has 20 male teachers. It has 30 female teachers. How many teachers are in the school?

   Are you to add or subtract? _____

   How many teachers are in the school? _____

   2.

3. Logan weighs 70 pounds. His older brother weighs 130 pounds. How many more pounds does his older brother weigh?

   Are you to add or subtract? _____

   How many more pounds does his older brother weigh? _____

   3.

   4.

4. Jessica has 110 pennies. Emily has 90 pennies. Jessica has how many more pennies than Emily?

   Jessica has _____ more pennies than Emily.

5. Mallory sold 50 pennants on Monday and 70 on Tuesday. How many pennants did she sell in all?

   Mallory sold _____ pennants in all.

   5.

   6.

6. A bag contains 150 red and green marbles. Ninety of them are red. How many marbles are green?

   _____ marbles are green.

Lesson 2 Addition (2-digit)

Add the ones.

$$\begin{array}{r} 43 \\ +86 \\ \hline \end{array}$$

$$\begin{array}{r} 43 \\ +86 \\ \hline 9 \end{array}$$

↑

$3 + 6 = 9$

Add the tens.

$$\begin{array}{r} 43 \\ +86 \\ \hline 129 \end{array}$$

$40 + 80 = 120$ or $100 + 20$

Add.

	a	b	c	d	e	f
1.	74 +62	56 +93	49 +60	57 +72	83 +35	94 +24
2.	62 +53	76 +72	34 +95	83 +43	96 +61	72 +41
3.	92 +30	74 +82	93 +92	86 +21	55 +60	34 +82
4.	65 +42	54 +82	83 +93	46 +90	93 +93	62 +64
5.	81 +58	65 +91	42 +84	35 +72	90 +70	80 +85
6.	93 +84	22 +97	45 +72	54 +54	43 +82	61 +81
7.	56 +82	62 +43	70 +76	54 +73	94 +94	85 +92

Lesson 2 Problem Solving

Solve each problem.

1. Austin sold 96 tickets. Carmen sold 81. How many tickets did they both sell?

   Austin sold _____ tickets.

   Carmen sold _____ tickets.

   They sold a total of _____ tickets.

2. Fifty-three people live in the first building. Eighty-five people live in the second building. How many people live in both buildings?

   _____ people live in the first building.

   _____ people live in the second building.

   _____ people live in both buildings.

3. A train went 83 kilometers the first hour. The second hour it went 84 kilometers. How far did it go in the two hours?

   The first hour
   the train went _____ kilometers.

   The second
   hour it went _____ kilometers.

   In the two
   hours it went _____ kilometers.

4. Ninety-two train seats are filled. There are 47 empty train seats. How many seats are on the train?

   There are _____ train seats.

5. Kara collected 72 stamps. Jan collected 76 stamps. How many stamps did they collect in all?

   They collected _____ stamps.

1.

2.

3.

4.   **5.**

Lesson 3   Subtraction (2- and 3-digit)

Subtract
the ones.

To subtract the tens,
rename 1 hundred and
3 tens as "13 tens."

Subtract
the tens.

$$\begin{array}{r} 136 \\ -72 \\ \hline \end{array}$$

$$\begin{array}{r} 136 \\ -72 \\ \hline 4 \end{array}$$

$$\begin{array}{r} ^{13}\!\!\!\not1\!3 6 \\ -72 \\ \hline 4 \end{array}$$

$$\begin{array}{r} ^{13}\!\!\!\not1\!3 6 \\ -72 \\ \hline 64 \end{array}$$

Subtract.

	a	b	c	d	e	f
1.	$\begin{array}{r}147\\-64\\\hline\end{array}$	$\begin{array}{r}108\\-72\\\hline\end{array}$	$\begin{array}{r}156\\-83\\\hline\end{array}$	$\begin{array}{r}129\\-44\\\hline\end{array}$	$\begin{array}{r}175\\-81\\\hline\end{array}$	$\begin{array}{r}114\\-42\\\hline\end{array}$
2.	$\begin{array}{r}136\\-86\\\hline\end{array}$	$\begin{array}{r}153\\-62\\\hline\end{array}$	$\begin{array}{r}118\\-91\\\hline\end{array}$	$\begin{array}{r}124\\-82\\\hline\end{array}$	$\begin{array}{r}136\\-43\\\hline\end{array}$	$\begin{array}{r}107\\-45\\\hline\end{array}$
3.	$\begin{array}{r}148\\-82\\\hline\end{array}$	$\begin{array}{r}164\\-83\\\hline\end{array}$	$\begin{array}{r}186\\-93\\\hline\end{array}$	$\begin{array}{r}115\\-72\\\hline\end{array}$	$\begin{array}{r}104\\-91\\\hline\end{array}$	$\begin{array}{r}146\\-52\\\hline\end{array}$
4.	$\begin{array}{r}107\\-23\\\hline\end{array}$	$\begin{array}{r}139\\-72\\\hline\end{array}$	$\begin{array}{r}124\\-30\\\hline\end{array}$	$\begin{array}{r}155\\-95\\\hline\end{array}$	$\begin{array}{r}166\\-72\\\hline\end{array}$	$\begin{array}{r}124\\-61\\\hline\end{array}$
5.	$\begin{array}{r}118\\-27\\\hline\end{array}$	$\begin{array}{r}126\\-55\\\hline\end{array}$	$\begin{array}{r}174\\-93\\\hline\end{array}$	$\begin{array}{r}149\\-72\\\hline\end{array}$	$\begin{array}{r}108\\-61\\\hline\end{array}$	$\begin{array}{r}136\\-94\\\hline\end{array}$
6.	$\begin{array}{r}145\\-92\\\hline\end{array}$	$\begin{array}{r}129\\-73\\\hline\end{array}$	$\begin{array}{r}152\\-72\\\hline\end{array}$	$\begin{array}{r}164\\-90\\\hline\end{array}$	$\begin{array}{r}135\\-62\\\hline\end{array}$	$\begin{array}{r}113\\-61\\\hline\end{array}$
7.	$\begin{array}{r}126\\-91\\\hline\end{array}$	$\begin{array}{r}185\\-94\\\hline\end{array}$	$\begin{array}{r}137\\-65\\\hline\end{array}$	$\begin{array}{r}158\\-86\\\hline\end{array}$	$\begin{array}{r}149\\-99\\\hline\end{array}$	$\begin{array}{r}176\\-83\\\hline\end{array}$

Lesson 3 Problem Solving

Solve each problem.

1. Rob had 128 centimeters of string. He used 73 centimeters of it. How much string was left?

   The string was _____ centimeters long.

   Rob used _____ centimeters of the string.

   There were _____ centimeters of string left.

2. Abby and Leigh got on a scale. The reading was 145 pounds. Leigh got off the scale, and the reading was 75 pounds. How much does Leigh weigh?

   Together they weigh _____ pounds.

   Abby weighs _____ pounds.

   Leigh weighs _____ pounds.

3. There are 167 students in Tony's grade at school. Seventy-one of the students are girls. How many of the students are boys?

   There are _____ students in all.

   There are _____ girls.

   There are _____ boys.

4. Brittnee had 156 sheets of paper in a package. Then she used 91 sheets. How many sheets of paper did she have left?

   She had _____ sheets of paper left.

5. A jet plane has 184 passenger seats. There are 93 passengers on the plane. How many empty passenger seats are there?

   There are _____ empty passenger seats.

1.	
2.	
3.	
4.	5.

Lesson 4 Addition and Subtraction (2- and 3-digit)

To check
75 + 61 = 136,
subtract _____
from 136.

$$\begin{array}{r} 75 \\ +61 \\ \hline 136 \\ -61 \\ \hline 75 \end{array}$$

These should
be the same.

To check
157 − 83 = 74,
add 83
to _____.

$$\begin{array}{r} 157 \\ -83 \\ \hline 74 \\ +83 \\ \hline 157 \end{array}$$

These should
be the same.

Add. Check each answer.

	a	*b*	*c*	*d*	*e*	*f*
1.	74 +53	85 +42	96 +60	43 +71	61 +45	32 +82
2.	91 +82	53 +63	96 +51	45 +82	32 +96	53 +51

Subtract. Check each answer.

3.	175 −83	156 −64	162 −91	189 −95	144 −60	128 −71
4.	136 −62	165 −83	157 −76	128 −61	147 −52	104 −21

Lesson 4 Problem Solving

Solve each problem.

1. Derrick worked at the computer for 80 minutes in the morning. That afternoon he worked at it for 40 minutes. How many minutes did he work on the computer that day?

Are you to add or subtract? _____

How many minutes did he work
on the computer that day? _____

1.

2. Derrick wrote a computer program with 129 lines. He has typed 91 lines of his program so far. How many more lines does he have to type?

Are you to add or subtract? _____

How many more lines
does he have to type? _____

2.

3. Derrick's mother uses the computer for work. Last month she used it 71 hours. This month she used it for 82 hours. How many hours did she use the computer in the last two months?

Are you to add or subtract? _____

How many hours did she use the
computer in the last two months? _____

3.

Lesson 5 Addition (2-digit)

Add the ones.   Add the tens.

$$58$$
$$+76$$

$$\overset{1}{5}8$$
$$+76$$
$$\overline{4}$$

$$\overset{1}{5}8$$
$$+76$$
$$\overline{134}$$

$8 + 6 = 14$ or $10 + 4$ $10 + 50 + 70 = 130$ or $100 + 30$

Add.

	a	b	c	d	e	f
1.	9 4 +6 8	7 7 +4 6	5 9 +7 5	7 2 +3 8	4 3 +9 9	6 6 +8 5
2.	8 7 +8 5	3 9 +9 2	6 6 +4 6	4 7 +7 8	7 5 +5 5	8 9 +9 6
3.	9 7 +5 9	8 9 +5 9	1 6 +9 5	3 4 +8 8	6 3 +9 8	9 9 +4 8
4.	3 7 +7 3	9 4 +2 8	9 9 +3 2	5 8 +9 5	6 7 +7 5	2 9 +8 5
5.	4 8 +8 6	6 9 +5 7	9 4 +9 7	7 2 +8 8	8 9 +6 4	8 7 +2 6
6.	5 4 +8 8	7 6 +7 6	8 9 +9 8	4 3 +6 8	9 6 +2 9	7 8 +6 8

Lesson 5 Problem Solving

Solve each problem.

1. A library loaned 74 books on Monday. It loaned 87 books on Tuesday. How many books did it loan on both days?

   The library loaned _____ books on Monday.

   The library loaned _____ books on Tuesday.

   The library loaned _____ books both days.

2. Barbara read 49 pages in the morning. She read 57 pages in the afternoon. How many pages did she read in all?

   Barbara read _____ pages in the morning.

   Barbara read _____ pages in the afternoon.

   Barbara read _____ pages in all.

3. The gym is 48 feet longer than the basketball court. The basketball court is 84 feet long. How long is the gym?

   The basketball court is _____ feet long.

   The gym is _____ feet longer than the basketball court.

   The gym is _____ feet long.

4. At the circus, 84 adult tickets and 96 child tickets were sold. How many tickets were sold?

   _____ tickets were sold.

5. The team scored 66 points in the first half. They scored 68 points in the second half. How many points did they score in the game?

   They scored _____ points in the game.

1.
2.
3.

4.	5.

Lesson 6   Subtraction (3-digit)

<table>
<tr><td>Rename 1 hundred and 6 ones as "10 tens and 6 ones."</td><td>Rename 10 tens and 6 ones as "9 tens and 16 ones."</td><td>Subtract the ones.</td><td>Subtract the tens.</td></tr>
<tr><td>106
−49</td><td>10
1̸0̸6
−49</td><td>9
10 16
1̸0̸6̸
−49</td><td>9
10 16
1̸0̸6̸
−49
   7</td><td>9
10 16
1̸0̸6̸
−49
 57</td></tr>
</table>

CHAPTER 5

Subtract.

	a	b	c	d	e	f
1.	135 −86	108 −19	113 −27	125 −48	142 −59	156 −88
2.	115 −78	122 −78	171 −99	140 −55	107 −18	132 −65
3.	186 −99	153 −65	132 −93	148 −79	115 −57	142 −64
4.	153 −95	104 −37	136 −48	150 −77	162 −95	174 −86
5.	143 −85	154 −96	163 −87	132 −75	120 −61	147 −78
6.	163 −99	174 −87	126 −58	142 −95	133 −58	114 −28
7.	102 −23	175 −97	166 −97	148 −59	133 −74	121 −98

Lesson 6 Problem Solving

Solve each problem.

1. Ms. Davis needs 180 meters of fence. She has 95 meters of fence. How many more meters of fence does she need?

   Ms. Davis needs _____ meters of fence.

   She has _____ meters of fence.

   She needs _____ more meters of fence.

   1.

2. Aaron knows the names of 128 students at school. If 79 are girls, how many are boys?

   Aaron knows the names of _____ students.

   _____ students are girls.

   _____ students are boys.

   2.

3. Margo's family is on a 162-kilometer trip. They have already gone 84 kilometers. How much farther do they have to go?

   The trip is _____ kilometers long.

   They have gone _____ kilometers.

   They have _____ more kilometers to go.

   3.

4. Ian's birthday is the 29th day of the year. Karen's birthday is the 126th day. Karen's birthday is how many days after Ian's birthday?

   Karen's birthday is _____ days after Ian's.

   4.

5. Mr. Darter bought 131 stamps at two post offices. He got 84 stamps at one post office. How many did he get at the other post office?

   Mr. Darter got _____ stamps.

   5.

Lesson 7 Addition and Subtraction (2- and 3-digit)

Add. Check each answer.

	a	*b*	*c*	*d*	*e*	*f*
1.	5 4 +3 8	7 1 +5 6	5 7 +8 6	9 5 +2 4	4 2 +3 7	5 8 +2 6
2.	7 2 +9 6	5 8 +7 4	9 2 +3 7	4 8 +2 2	3 5 +4 3	5 5 +5 5

Subtract. Check each answer.

	a	*b*	*c*	*d*	*e*	*f*
3.	1 2 5 −9 2	1 7 4 −3 3	1 6 5 −8 7	1 5 0 −9 0	1 4 6 −7 6	1 3 2 −8 4
4.	1 1 2 −4 7	1 1 8 −3 3	1 5 7 −2 6	1 6 0 −4 5	1 7 5 −7 6	1 5 3 −8 3
5.	1 9 8 −3 9	1 5 5 −9 7	1 6 3 −8 4	1 3 1 −7 1	1 1 1 −2 4	1 0 8 −3 9

Lesson 7   Problem Solving

Solve each problem.

1. There are 166 people living in my apartment
   building. If 98 are children, how many are adults?

   There are _____ people in the building.

   There are _____ children.

   There are _____ adults.

2. There were 115 cases on a truck. The driver left
   27 cases at the first stop. How many cases are still
   on the truck?

   _____ cases were on a truck.

   _____ cases were left at the first stop.

   _____ cases are still on the truck.

3. The bus has 84 passenger seats. All the seats are
   filled, and there are 39 passengers standing. How
   many passengers are on the bus?

   The bus has _____ seats.

   There are _____ passengers standing.

   There are _____ passengers on the bus.

4. Breanne counted 63 houses on one side of the
   street. She counted 89 on the other side. How
   many houses are on the street?

   There are _____ houses on the street.

5. Lindsay had 112 balloons. She gave some of them
   away. She had 35 balloons left. How many balloons
   did she give away?

   She gave away _____ balloons.

1.

2.

3.

4.

5.

CHAPTER 5 PRACTICE TEST
Addition and Subtraction (2- and 3-digit; with renaming)

Add or subtract. Check each answer.

	a	*b*	*c*	*d*	*e*
1.	60 +80	70 +90	85 +63	72 +54	60 +65
2.	84 +57	63 +77	82 +99	78 +78	44 +79
3.	170 −80	160 −80	153 −71	127 −82	175 −91
4.	127 −59	143 −65	166 −89	183 −95	122 −57
5.	147 −36	56 +37	175 −85	57 +89	197 −73

CHAPTER 6 PRETEST
Addition and Subtraction (2-, 3-, and 4-digit; with renaming)

Add.

	a	b	c	d	e	f
1.	3 4 +7	8 6 +9	9 5 +7	5 6 8 +3	4 9 2 +6	3 7 5 +9
2.	10 30 40 +50	20 30 40 +60	20 40 60 +70	40 30 80 +40	50 50 20 +60	20 60 20 +40
3.	52 41 +30	26 30 +92	33 44 +57	38 46 +69	49 65 +77	27 34 +46
4.	23 23 31 +22	28 17 23 +44	91 22 34 +51	72 54 36 +21	78 52 43 +45	33 25 36 +21
5.	423 101 +324	526 345 +116	123 541 +162	752 348 +150	429 316 541 +302	324 115 462 +115

Subtract.

	a	b	c	d	e
6.	752 −341	673 −424	583 −193	765 −489	605 −329
7.	4723 −221	5806 −447	3924 −163	7811 −912	6425 −587

Lesson 1 Addition (three or more numbers)

	Add the ones.		Add the tens.

```
   67            7              →1          67              1
   98            8  >15                      98             67
  +83           +3    +3    │   │          +83             98
  ─────         ──   ──     │   │          ─────          +83
                     18 or 10 + 8    8                    ─────
                              └─ ─ ─ →↑                    248
```

Add.

	a	b	c	d	e	f
1.	4 5 + 7	6 8 + 9	5 2 + 8	9 8 + 3	4 6 + 5	7 7 + 6
2.	1 0 4 0 3 0 + 5 0	2 0 6 0 5 0 + 6 0	1 0 2 0 9 0 + 4 0	2 0 4 0 3 0 + 7 0	1 0 5 0 6 0 + 4 0	2 0 7 0 5 0 + 8 0
3.	4 4 3 5 + 5 7	6 6 5 8 + 5 9	2 5 9 2 + 4 8	4 9 3 8 + 7 3	5 4 6 6 + 4 5	7 7 5 7 + 8 6
4.	2 5 3 2 + 4 1	2 7 3 5 + 4 2	5 5 5 5 + 5 5	3 2 4 4 + 2 8	7 5 1 6 + 5 8	2 2 1 4 + 9 1
5.	5 7 2 8 + 3 6	4 2 5 4 + 7 8	7 9 3 4 + 2 9	6 8 7 8 + 8 8	2 5 3 6 + 4 2	5 3 2 6 + 1 3
6.	4 5 1 8 + 5 2	6 1 2 9 + 5 8	8 3 7 6 + 1 9	4 9 4 2 + 4 3	3 7 6 7 + 2 6	9 8 1 6 + 3 5

CHAPTER 6

Lesson 1 Problem Solving

NATIONAL LEAGUE TEAM STANDINGS		
TEAM	WON	LOST
CUBS	72	43
CARDINALS	69	48
METS	64	52
PIRATES	58	55
PHILLIES	44	68
EXPOS	37	79

Solve each problem.

1. How many games have been won by the first three teams in the National League?

The Cubs have won _____ games.

The Cardinals have won _____ games.

The Mets have won _____ games.

Together they have won _____ games.

1.

2. How many games have been lost by the last three teams in the National League?

The Pirates have lost _____ games.

The Phillies have lost _____ games.

The Expos have lost _____ games.

Together they have lost _____ games.

2.

3. How many games have been won by the Cubs, Mets, Phillies, and Expos?

They have won _____ games.

3.   **4.**

4. How many games have the Cubs, Cardinals, and Pirates lost?

They have lost _____ games.

Lesson 2 Addition (three or more numbers)

	Add the ones.	**Add the tens.**	Add the hundreds.

		1	2 1	2 1
	642	642	642	642
	156	156	156	156
	275	275	275	275
	+143	+143	+143	+143
		6	16	1216

$2 + 6 + 5 + 3 =$ ___ | $10 + 40 + 50 + 70 + 40 =$ ____ | $200 + 600 + 100 + 200 + 100 =$ ____

$16 = 10 +$ _____ | $210 = 200 +$ _____ | $1200 = 1000 +$ _____

Add.

	a	b	c	d	e	f
1.	3 7 2 4 5 6 +1 7 4	3 8 2 1 5 4 +2 8 3	2 3 1 3 3 6 +1 3 6	1 5 2 4 4 3 +1 7 8	3 2 1 3 0 5 +2 3 8	1 4 3 1 1 6 +2 1 2
2.	4 2 5 6 4 1 +7 0 3	4 4 3 2 1 7 +6 0 2	6 1 3 2 4 7 +1 3 8	5 7 4 1 4 2 +2 8 1	3 8 2 4 2 5 +6 7 8	3 9 2 4 5 6 +7 3 1
3.	7 2 8 3 6 5 +4 2 8	6 3 9 7 5 2 +4 1 7	6 1 8 3 0 4 +1 2 0	8 5 6 1 7 4 +3 7 2	5 6 4 3 4 5 +6 5 4	2 2 4 3 0 5 +4 0 6
4.	4 2 1 1 4 5 1 6 2 +2 3 1	1 7 8 2 1 4 1 0 3 +4 0 7	5 1 3 2 2 3 6 4 1 +4 1 2	4 2 1 1 4 6 2 7 3 +1 5 4	7 6 2 5 3 1 4 4 4 +2 5 8	3 7 2 5 4 1 6 3 5 +4 1 3
5.	6 0 3 2 5 4 3 1 6 +2 2 2	4 2 5 2 4 5 5 4 2 +2 5 4	6 3 1 2 1 1 4 3 1 +2 2 2	7 3 1 2 4 0 6 3 5 +2 1 4	2 4 5 3 6 1 5 2 4 +1 1 3	2 8 4 5 6 3 7 1 1 +2 4 5

CHAPTER 6

Lesson 2 Problem Solving

Solve each problem.

1. The local theater had a special Saturday movie. They sold 175 tickets to men, 142 to women, and 327 to children. How many tickets did they sell in all?

They sold _____ tickets to men.

They sold _____ tickets to women.

They sold _____ tickets to children.

They sold _____ tickets in all.

2. In the local high school there are 768 boys, 829 girls, and 107 teachers. How many teachers and students are there in all?

There are _____ boys.

There are _____ girls.

There are _____ teachers.

There are _____ teachers and students in all.

3. The following numbers of people live in four different apartment buildings: 203, 245, 268, and 275. How many people live in all four buildings?

_____ people live in all four buildings.

4. A living room floor has 195 tiles. A bedroom floor has 168 tiles. A kitchen floor has 144 tiles. How many tiles are in these three rooms?

There are _____ tiles in these three rooms.

1.

2.

3.   **4.**

Lesson 3 Subtraction (3-digit)

Rename 40 as "3 tens and 10 ones." Then subtract the ones.

Rename 7 hundreds and 3 tens as "6 hundreds and 13 tens." Then subtract the tens.

Subtract the hundreds.

```
    740          3 10          13           13
                 740         6 3 10        6 3 10
   -271         -271          740           740
                ----         -271          -271
                   9         ----          ----
                               69           469
```

Subtract.

	a	b	c	d	e	f
1.	534 −273	263 −154	758 −439	450 −261	536 −347	274 −154
2.	463 −372	782 −234	594 −287	681 −382	384 −175	806 −764
3.	764 −137	635 −447	492 −113	780 −152	444 −235	562 −357
4.	836 −257	944 −256	758 −167	504 −235	672 −285	892 −284
5.	945 −463	378 −126	564 −243	839 −257	245 −146	776 −382
6.	805 −308	900 −750	764 −345	840 −426	955 −765	436 −327

Lesson 3 Problem Solving

Solve each problem.

1. Babe Ruth hit 714 home runs. Henry (Hank) Aaron hit 755 home runs. How many more home runs did Hank Aaron hit than Babe Ruth?

   Babe Ruth hit _____ home runs.

   Hank Aaron hit _____ home runs.

   Hank Aaron hit _____ more home runs than Babe Ruth.

1.

2. A train has 850 seats. There are 317 empty seats. How many people are seated?

   The train has _____ seats.

   _____ seats are empty.

   There are _____ people seated.

2.

3. Hoover Dam is 726 feet high. Folsom Dam is 340 feet high. How much higher is Hoover Dam than Folsom Dam?

   Hoover Dam is _____ feet high.

   Folsom Dam is _____ feet high.

   Hoover Dam is _____ feet higher than Folsom Dam.

3.

4. The quarterback threw 247 passes. Only 138 passes were caught. How many were not caught?

   _____ passes were not caught.

4.

5. A meeting room can hold 443 people. There are 268 people in the room now. How many more people can it hold?

   The meeting room can hold _____ more people.

5.

Lesson 4 Subtraction (3- and 4-digit)

	Subtract the ones.	Rename 2 hundreds and 5 tens as "1 hundred and 15 tens." Subtract the tens.	Rename 4 thousands and 1 hundred as "3 thousands and 11 hundreds." Subtract the hundreds.	Subtract the thousands.

$$\begin{array}{r} 4253 \\ -281 \\ \hline \end{array} \qquad \begin{array}{r} 4253 \\ -281 \\ \hline 2 \end{array} \qquad \begin{array}{r} {}^{1\,15} \\ 42\cancel{5}3 \\ -281 \\ \hline 72 \end{array} \qquad \begin{array}{r} {}^{11} \\ 3\cancel{4}15 \\ 42\cancel{5}3 \\ -281 \\ \hline 972 \end{array} \qquad \begin{array}{r} {}^{11} \\ 3\cancel{4}15 \\ 42\cancel{5}3 \\ -281 \\ \hline 3972 \end{array}$$

Subtract.

	a	b	c	d	e
1.	7543 −211	6813 −402	7254 −132	4936 −726	2815 −813
2.	3562 −235	4253 −147	6541 −538	3473 −255	5496 −339
3.	3710 −340	9642 −271	3817 −454	5216 −182	3847 −377
4.	4295 −724	4007 −805	8281 −470	5554 −644	6382 −882
5.	5986 −537	2413 −829	4507 −758	3154 −205	2604 −834
6.	8329 −475	7604 −829	3987 −988	4205 −736	1383 −529

Lesson 4 Problem Solving

Solve each problem.

1. Ms. Ramos bought a car that cost 3,165 dollars. She paid 875 dollars. How much does she still owe?

The new car cost _____ dollars.

Ms. Ramos paid _____ dollars.

She still owes _____ dollars.

2. Mount Whitney is 4,418 meters high. Mount Davis is 979 meters high. How much higher is Mount Whitney?

Mount Whitney is _____ meters high.

Mount Davis is _____ meters high.

Mount Whitney is _____ meters higher.

3. There are 1,156 students enrolled in a school. Today 219 students are absent. How many are present?

_____ students are present.

4. There are 5,280 feet in a mile. John walked 895 feet. How many more feet must he go to walk a mile?

He must go _____ more feet to walk a mile.

5. Albertito's family went 2,198 kilometers in 5 days. They went 843 kilometers the first 2 days. How many kilometers did they go in the last 3 days?

They went _____ kilometers in the last three days.

6. There are 1,255 people on a police force. If 596 are women, how many are men?

There are _____ men.

1.

2.

3.

4.

5.

6.

Lesson 5 Estimation

Round each number to the highest place value the numbers have in common. Then add from right to left.

$$
\begin{array}{r}
124 \\
+\ 268
\end{array}
\longrightarrow
\begin{array}{r}
100 \\
+\ 300 \\
\hline
400
\end{array}
$$

Round each number to the highest place value the numbers have in common. Then subtract from right to left.

$$
\begin{array}{r}
879 \\
-\ 42
\end{array}
\longrightarrow
\begin{array}{r}
880 \\
-\ 40 \\
\hline
840
\end{array}
$$

Estimate each sum or difference.

	a	b	c	d	e
1.	$\begin{array}{r} 35 \\ +88 \end{array}$	$\begin{array}{r} 74 \\ +36 \end{array}$	$\begin{array}{r} 12 \\ +48 \end{array}$	$\begin{array}{r} 89 \\ +91 \end{array}$	$\begin{array}{r} 28 \\ +52 \end{array}$
2.	$\begin{array}{r} 67 \\ -23 \end{array}$	$\begin{array}{r} 24 \\ -19 \end{array}$	$\begin{array}{r} 44 \\ -31 \end{array}$	$\begin{array}{r} 61 \\ -46 \end{array}$	$\begin{array}{r} 54 \\ -33 \end{array}$
3.	$\begin{array}{r} 158 \\ -102 \end{array}$	$\begin{array}{r} 279 \\ -46 \end{array}$	$\begin{array}{r} 674 \\ -512 \end{array}$	$\begin{array}{r} 382 \\ -224 \end{array}$	$\begin{array}{r} 429 \\ -129 \end{array}$
4.	$\begin{array}{r} 348 \\ +289 \end{array}$	$\begin{array}{r} 628 \\ +314 \end{array}$	$\begin{array}{r} 942 \\ +546 \end{array}$	$\begin{array}{r} 376 \\ +296 \end{array}$	$\begin{array}{r} 466 \\ +423 \end{array}$
5.	$\begin{array}{r} 6752 \\ -5201 \end{array}$	$\begin{array}{r} 1238 \\ -456 \end{array}$	$\begin{array}{r} 6219 \\ -338 \end{array}$	$\begin{array}{r} 3062 \\ -786 \end{array}$	$\begin{array}{r} 5008 \\ -3460 \end{array}$

CHAPTER 6

Lesson 5 Problem Solving

Solve each problem.

1. On Sunday Jamie ate three meals. Her breakfast had 378 calories. Her lunch contained 556 calories. Her dinner had 612 calories. About how many calories did Jamie take in on Sunday?

   Are you to add or subtract? _____

   About how many calories did Jamie take in on Sunday?

   about _____ calories

2. The doctor suggested that Jamie take in about 1,800 calories each day. About how many more calories could Jamie have taken in that Sunday?

   Are you to add or subtract? _____

   About how many more calories could Jamie have taken in on Sunday?

   about _____ calories

3. Antonio read 102 pages of a book on Monday. On Tuesday he read 67 pages. About how many fewer pages did he read on Tuesday than on Monday?

   Are you to add or subtract? _____

   About how many fewer pages did Antonio read on Tuesday than on Monday?

   about _____ pages

4. The third grade at Elm Grade School went on a field trip. Two school buses were filled with children. One bus had 72 children on it and the other bus was carrying 81 children. About how many children went on the field trip?

   Are you to add or subtract? _____

   About how many children went on the field trip?

   about _____ children

| 1. |
| 2. |
| 3. |
| 4. |

Lesson 6   Number Patterns

Look at the set of numbers. Find the pattern and then name the next three numbers in the set.

$$5, 8, 11, 14, \underline{\quad}, \underline{\quad}, \underline{\quad}$$

To get from 5 to 8, add 3.

To get from 8 to 11, add 3.

To get from 11 to 14, add 3.

The pattern is to **add 3.**

$$5, 8, 11, 14, \underline{17}, \underline{20}, \underline{23}$$

Find the pattern and then name the next three numbers in the set.

$$112, 102, 92, 82, \underline{\quad}, \underline{\quad}, \underline{\quad}$$

To get from 112 to 102, subtract 10.

To get from 102 to 92, subtract 10.

To get from 92 to 82, subtract 10.

The pattern is to **subtract 10.**

$$112, 102, 92, 82, \underline{72}, \underline{62}, \underline{52}$$

Find the number pattern. Write the missing numbers.

	a	*b*
1.	2, 4, 6, ___, ___, ___	25, 20, 15, ___, ___, ___
2.	21, 24, 27, ___, ___, ___	125, 100, 75, ___, ___, ___
3.	8, 13, 18, ___, ___, ___	19, 17, 15, ___, ___, ___
4.	1, 3, 5, ___, ___, ___	66, 55, 44, ___, ___, ___
5.	32, 34, 36, ___, ___, ___	90, 87, 84, ___, ___, ___
6.	1, 5, 9, ___, ___, ___	51, 50, 49, ___, ___, ___

Lesson 6 Problem Solving

Solve each problem.

1. Kenesha made $45 from her garage sale on Wednesday. On Thursday, she made $40. On Friday, she made $35. If her sales continue with this pattern, how much money can she expect to make on Saturday?

   Does the pattern increase or decrease?
   _____

   What is the relationship in the pattern?
   _____

   How much can Kenesha expect to make on Saturday? _____

2. William and Marcus collect aluminum cans from the nearby park on Mondays, Wednesdays, and Saturdays. On each collection day, they add 20 cans to their total. Their total before Monday is 130. What will their new total be at the end of the week?

   What is the total after Monday's collection? _____ cans

   What is the total after Wednesday's collection? _____ cans

   What is the total after Saturday's collection? _____ cans

3. The Jones family is packing to move to a new house. At the end of the first day of packing, 8 boxes are ready. At the end of the second day, 16 boxes are ready. By the end of the third day, 24 boxes are ready. If they continue to pack at the same rate, how many boxes will be packed by the sixth packing day?

   How many boxes are ready at the end of the fourth day? _____ boxes

   How many boxes are ready at the end of the fifth day? _____ boxes

   How many boxes will be ready at the end of the sixth day? _____ boxes

1.

2.

3.

CHAPTER 6 PRACTICE TEST
Addition and Subtraction (2-, 3-, and 4-digit; with renaming)

Add.

	a	*b*	*c*	*d*	*e*
1.	3 2 + 5	3 5 2 4 + 2 0	5 7 1 3 + 2 8	7 0 3 0 8 0 + 4 0	4 2 5 3 6 4 + 7 0
2.	4 2 1 3 1 2 + 1 4 8	6 2 3 1 7 4 + 1 6 2	4 7 3 1 2 6 + 2 4 8	3 2 6 1 1 2 2 2 4 + 6 0 7	5 2 6 3 8 1 4 2 6 + 5 4 3

Subtract.

	a	*b*	*c*	*d*	*e*
3.	7 6 5 − 2 4 3	2 9 0 − 1 8 3	8 4 6 − 3 5 4	2 5 6 0 − 7 6 4	7 5 4 2 − 2 7 5

Estimate the sum or difference.

	a	*b*	*c*	*d*	*e*
4.	8 5 + 4 1	4 9 + 1 4 5	3 2 7 + 2 1 6	6 1 4 9 + 7 8 2	6 0 8 + 9 5 6
5.	6 3 − 2 7	2 4 7 − 1 8 6	8 8 − 1 8	9 0 0 2 − 1 5 5 7	5 4 2 − 6 6

Find the number pattern. Write the missing numbers.

	a	*b*	*c*
6.	12, 10, 8, ___, ___, ___	15, 35, 55, ___, ___, ___	101, 111, 121, ___, ___, ___

Solve.

7. Four girls earned the following points in a contest: 145, 387, 245, and 197. What was the total number of points earned?

The estimated total number of points is about _____.

The total number of points was _____.

7.

CHAPTER 7 PRETEST
Time and Money

Complete the following.

	a	b
1.	There are _____ days in a year.	4:10 means 10 minutes after _____.
2.	There are _____ days in a leap year.	3:50 means 10 minutes to _____.
3.	There are _____ days in April.	5:45 means _____ minutes after 5.
4.	There are _____ days in March.	5:45 means _____ minutes to 6.

Complete the following as shown.

	a	b	c
5.	XI = ___11___	V = _____	IV = _____
6.	XVII = _____	XXVI = _____	XIX = _____
7.	7 = ___VII___	10 = _____	9 = _____
8.	24 = _____	31 = _____	25 = _____

Add or subtract.

	a	b	c	d	e
9.	$5.2 0 +6.8 9	$1 2.6 5 +1.2 5	4 6¢ +3 7¢	2 9¢ 3 7¢ +2 8¢	$1 4.5 0 0.2 8 +3.7 3
10.	$1 6.5 0 −3.2 5	$1 4.7 5 −2.9 0	$7.4 0 −0.8 4	5 6¢ −3 8¢	9 7¢ −5 0¢

Solve.

11. Ms. Romanez bought a saw for $21.95 and a hammer for $9.49. She paid $1.88 tax. How much was her total bill?

11.

Her total bill was _____.

Lesson 1   Reading Our Calendar

January	February	March	April
S M T W T F S	S M T W T F S	S M T W T F S	S M T W T F S
1	1 2 3 4 5	1 2 3 4 5	1 2
2 3 4 5 6 7 8	6 7 8 9 10 11 12	6 7 8 9 10 11 12	3 4 5 6 7 8 9
9 10 11 12 13 14 15	13 14 15 16 17 18 19	13 14 15 16 17 18 19	10 11 12 13 14 15 16
16 17 18 19 20 21 22	20 21 22 23 24 25 26	20 21 22 23 24 25 26	17 18 19 20 21 22 23
23 24 25 26 27 28 29	27 28	27 28 29 30 31	24 25 26 27 28 29 30
30 31			

May	June	July	August
S M T W T F S	S M T W T F S	S M T W T F S	S M T W T F S
1 2 3 4 5 6 7	1 2 3 4	1 2	1 2 3 4 5 6
8 9 10 11 12 13 14	5 6 7 8 9 10 11	3 4 5 6 7 8 9	7 8 9 10 11 12 13
15 16 17 18 19 20 21	12 13 14 15 16 17 18	10 11 12 13 14 15 16	14 15 16 17 18 19 20
22 23 24 25 26 27 28	19 20 21 22 23 24 25	17 18 19 20 21 22 23	21 22 23 24 25 26 27
29 30 31	26 27 28 29 30	24 25 26 27 28 29 30	28 29 30 31
		31	

September	October	November	December
S M T W T F S	S M T W T F S	S M T W T F S	S M T W T F S
1 2 3	1	1 2 3 4 5	1 2 3
4 5 6 7 8 9 10	2 3 4 5 6 7 8	6 7 8 9 10 11 12	4 5 6 7 8 9 10
11 12 13 14 15 16 17	9 10 11 12 13 14 15	13 14 15 16 17 18 19	11 12 13 14 15 16 17
18 19 20 21 22 23 24	16 17 18 19 20 21 22	20 21 22 23 24 25 26	18 19 20 21 22 23 24
25 26 27 28 29 30	23 24 25 26 27 28 29	27 28 29 30	25 26 27 28 29 30 31
	30 31		

There are 365 days in the calendar year shown. Every four years, there are 366 days in a year. It is called a **leap year.** Only in a leap year is there a February 29.

There are ____31____ days in March.   There are _____ days in June.

March 1 is on ____Tuesday____.   June 1 is on _____.

On the calendar above, April has __4__ Sundays and _____ Saturdays.

Answer each question. Use the calendar to help you.

a   b

1. How many days are in July? _____   On what day is July 1? _____

2. How many Tuesdays are in November? _____   How many Wednesdays are in November? _____

3. How many months have exactly 30 days? _____   How many months have 31 days? _____

4. What date is the third Thursday in August? _____   What date is the second Monday in April? _____

5. How many days of the year have passed when we reach May 1? _____   What date falls 45 days before December 25? _____

Lesson 2 Telling Time

 { 7:10 is read "seven ten" and means "10 minutes after 7."

7:10

 { 3:40 is read "three forty" and means "40 minutes after 3" or "20 minutes to 4."

3:40

 { 8:55 is read "eight fifty-five" and means "55 minutes after _____" or "_____ minutes to _____."

8:55

Complete the following.

		a		b
1.	3:05 means _____ minutes after _____.		6:50 means _____ minutes to _____.
2.	10:20 means _____ minutes after _____.		11:35 means _____ minutes to _____.
3.	8:45 means _____ minutes after _____.		8:45 means _____ minutes to _____.
4.	5:30 means _____ minutes after _____.		5:30 means _____ minutes to _____.
5.	1:10 means _____ minutes after _____.		12:55 means _____ minutes to _____.

For each clock face, write the numerals that name the time.

	a	b	c	d

6.

_____ : _____   _____ : _____   _____ : _____   _____ : _____

7.

_____ : _____   _____ : _____   _____ : _____   _____ : _____

Lesson 3 Roman Numerals

I means 1.   V means 5.   X means 10.

II means 1 + 1 or 2.   III means 1 + 1 + 1 or 3.

VI means 5 + 1 or 6.   IV means 5 − 1 or 4.

XXV means 10 + 10 + 5 or 25.   IX means 10 − 1 or 9.

VII means 5 + 1 + _____ or _____.   XXI means 10 + _____ + 1 or _____.

XIV means _____ + 4 or _____.   XIX means _____ + 9 or _____.

Complete the following as shown.

	a	b	c	d
1.	XXIV = 24	XX = _____	XII = _____	VIII = _____
2.	IV = _____	XXVI = _____	XVII = _____	XXXI = _____
3.	XXXVI = _____	XXIX = _____	XI = _____	XXXIII = _____
4.	XVIII = _____	IX = _____	XXXIV = _____	XIII = _____
5.	V = _____	XXV = _____	VI = _____	XXI = _____
6.	XXXVIII = _____	XXXV = _____	XXVII = _____	XVI = _____
7.	XXIII = _____	XXXVII = _____	XIV = _____	XXXII = _____

Write a Roman numeral for each of the following.

	a	b	c
8.	3 = _____	7 = _____	15 = _____
9.	19 = _____	22 = _____	28 = _____
10.	30 = _____	20 = _____	39 = _____

Lesson 4   Money

1 penny	1 nickel	1 dime	1 quarter	1 dollar
1 cent	5 cents	10 cents	25 cents	100 cents
1¢ or $0.01	5¢ or $0.05	10¢ or $0.10	25¢ or $0.25	$1.00

25 pennies have a value of ____25____ cents or ____1____ quarter.

5 pennies have a value of _____ cents or _____ nickel.

$2.57 means ____2____ dollars and ____57____ cents.

$3.45 means _____ dollars and _____ cents.

Complete the following.

1. 10 pennies have a value of _____ cents or _____ nickels.

2. 10 pennies have a value of _____ cents or _____ dime.

3. 20 pennies have a value of _____ cents or _____ dimes.

4. 15 pennies have a value of _____ cents or _____ nickels.

5. 20 pennies have a value of _____ cents or _____ nickels.

Complete the following as shown.

6. $14.05 means ____14____ dollars and ____5____ cents.

7. $12.70 means _____ dollars and _____ cents.

8. $8.14 means _____ dollars and _____ cents.

9. $0.65 means _____ dollars and _____ cents.

10. $10.01 means _____ dollars and _____ cent.

Lesson 5 Addition and Subtraction of Money

	$12.00				
$9.05	0.45	45¢	$0.75	$14.08	$13.00
+6.98	+3.16	+38¢	+0.38	−7.25	−6.05
$16.03	$15.61	83¢	$1.13	$6.83	$6.95

Add or subtract as usual.

Put a decimal point (.) and a $ or ¢ in the answer.

Be sure to line up the decimal points.

Add or subtract.

	a	b	c	d	e
1.	$ 0.3 6 +12.4 0	$3.7 5 +1.4 6	$ 1.3 6 +40.0 0	3 7¢ +5 8¢	$4.3 5 +0.2 7
2.	$5.2 0 −3.1 8	$1 2.6 4 −5.0 8	$3.0 0 −0.5 4	8 8¢ −7 6¢	$2 4.4 2 −1.6 8
3.	$ 4.2 3 1 6.9 0 +0.8 9	$7.2 5 0.4 0 +4.4 2	$ 8.0 5 1 2.1 6 +0.5 8	4 7¢ 1 8¢ +2 5¢	$ 0.0 8 3.6 7 +14.3 0
4.	$1 5.4 0 −3.6 2	$ 5.7 0 −2.0 8	$1 1.3 0 −0.8 6	9 1¢ −7 5¢	$1 7.2 0 −4.0 6
5.	$2 7.0 0 −1 3.4 5	$6 5.2 1 +3.8 0	$0.1 2 +1.8 8	4 7¢ −1 9¢	$3.0 0 −1.7 8
6.	$1 6.4 9 +2 8.9 8	$4 0.6 0 −7.5 6	$5.0 0 −2.7 2	3 8¢ +3 5¢	$8.7 5 +0.6 4

Lesson 5   Problem Solving

Solve each problem.

1. Caitlin's mother bought a dress for $22.98 and a blouse for $17.64. How much did these items cost in all?

   They cost _____ in all.

2. Find the total cost of a basketball at $18.69, a baseball at $8.05, and a football at $24.98.

   The total cost is _____.

3. Jeremy has $2.50. Landon has $1.75. Jeremy has how much more money than Landon?

   Jeremy has _____ more than Landon.

4. In problem **2,** how much more does the basketball cost than the baseball? How much more does the football cost than the basketball?

   The basketball costs _____ more than the baseball.

   The football costs _____ more than the basketball.

5. Alexandra saved $4.20 one week, $0.90 the next week, and $2.05 the third week. How much money did she save during these three weeks?

   Alexandra saved _____ in three weeks.

6. Mr. Lewis paid $4.45 for fruit. He paid $0.99 for potatoes. The tax was $0.33. How much was the total bill?

   His total bill was _____.

7. Tyler wants to buy a 95¢ whistle. He now has 68¢. How much more money does he need to buy the whistle?

   Tyler needs _____ more.

1.

2.

3.

4.

5.

6.

7.

CHAPTER 7 PRACTICE TEST
Time and Money

Answer each question. Use the calendar.

			May			
S	M	T	W	T	F	S
		1	2	3	4	5
6	7	8	9	10	11	12
13	14	15	16	17	18	19
20	21	22	23	24	25	26
27	28	29	30	31		

1. How many days are in May? _____

2. On what day is May 4? _____

For each clock face, write the numerals that name the time.

        a   *b*   *c*

3.

_____ : _____   _____ : _____   _____ : _____

Complete the following as shown.

        a   *b*   *c*

4. XVI = _____16_____   IX = _____   XXXII = _____

5. 14 = _____XIV_____   8 = _____   29 = _____

Add or subtract.

	a	*b*	*c*	*d*	*e*
6.	$15.32 +16.45	$3.24 +0.73	42¢ +54¢	16¢ 37¢ +20¢	$13.40 0.62 +1.68
7.	$3.52 −2.17	$13.14 −5.33	93¢ −39¢	$17.50 −1.09	$5.14 −1.08

Solve.

8. Maria needs $54.68 to buy a coat she wants. She now has $50.75. How much more money does she need to buy the coat?

Maria needs _____ more.

8.

CHAPTER 8 PRETEST
Multiplication (basic facts through 5 × 9)

Multiply.

	a	b	c	d	e	f
1.	5 ×2	7 ×2	2 ×2	6 ×2	4 ×2	9 ×2
2.	3 ×3	5 ×3	4 ×3	7 ×3	9 ×3	2 ×3
3.	7 ×0	5 ×0	0 ×4	0 ×6	3 ×0	0 ×8
4.	3 ×1	7 ×1	1 ×4	1 ×1	5 ×1	1 ×8
5.	7 ×4	3 ×4	9 ×4	6 ×4	5 ×4	4 ×4
6.	8 ×5	6 ×5	9 ×5	4 ×5	3 ×5	2 ×5
7.	9 ×0	8 ×4	6 ×3	0 ×1	5 ×5	0 ×3
8.	1 ×9	2 ×4	1 ×2	7 ×5	8 ×3	2 ×1
9.	3 ×2	1 ×3	0 ×7	8 ×2	1 ×6	1 ×5

Lesson 1 Multiplication (introduction)

2 × 3 is read "two times three."   2 × 3 means 3 + 3.
3 × 2 is read "three times two."   3 × 2 means 2 + 2 + 2.
4 × 5 is read "four times five."   4 × 5 means 5 + 5 + 5 + 5.

3 × 6 is read "three times six."   3 × 6 means _____.

2 × 7 is read "two times seven."   2 × 7 means _____.

Complete the following as shown.

1. 2 × 5 is read _____ "two times five" _____.

2. 3 × 4 is read _____.

3. 5 × 2 is read _____.

4. 4 × 8 is read _____.

5. 4 × 7 is read _____.

Complete the following as shown.

	a		*b*

6. 2 × 4 means _____ 4 + 4 _____.   4 × 2 means _____ 2 + 2 + 2 + 2 _____.

7. 3 × 5 means _____.   5 × 3 means _____.

8. 3 × 7 means _____.   7 × 3 means _____.

9. 4 × 6 means _____.   6 × 4 means _____.

10. 2 × 8 means _____.   8 × 2 means _____.

11. 3 × 9 means _____.   9 × 3 means _____.

Lesson 2 Multiplication (concept)

3×4 means $4 + 4 + 4$. 4×3 means $3 + 3 + 3 + 3$.

$$\begin{array}{r} 4 \\ \times 3 \\ \hline 12 \end{array} \qquad \begin{array}{r} 4 \\ 4 \\ +4 \\ \hline 12 \end{array} \qquad \begin{array}{r} 3 \\ \times 4 \\ \hline 12 \end{array} \qquad \begin{array}{r} 3 \\ 3 \\ 3 \\ +3 \\ \hline 12 \end{array}$$

Add or multiply.

	a	*b*	*c*	*d*	*e*	*f*
1.	$\begin{array}{r} 8 \\ +8 \\ \hline \end{array}$	$\begin{array}{r} 8 \\ \times 2 \\ \hline \end{array}$	$\begin{array}{r} 4 \\ +4 \\ \hline \end{array}$	$\begin{array}{r} 4 \\ \times 2 \\ \hline \end{array}$	$\begin{array}{r} 5 \\ +5 \\ \hline \end{array}$	$\begin{array}{r} 5 \\ \times 2 \\ \hline \end{array}$
2.	$\begin{array}{r} 6 \\ +6 \\ \hline \end{array}$	$\begin{array}{r} 6 \\ \times 2 \\ \hline \end{array}$	$\begin{array}{r} 7 \\ +7 \\ \hline \end{array}$	$\begin{array}{r} 7 \\ \times 2 \\ \hline \end{array}$	$\begin{array}{r} 2 \\ +2 \\ \hline \end{array}$	$\begin{array}{r} 2 \\ \times 2 \\ \hline \end{array}$
3.	$\begin{array}{r} 9 \\ +9 \\ \hline \end{array}$	$\begin{array}{r} 9 \\ \times 2 \\ \hline \end{array}$	$\begin{array}{r} 3 \\ +3 \\ \hline \end{array}$	$\begin{array}{r} 3 \\ \times 2 \\ \hline \end{array}$	$\begin{array}{r} 1 \\ +1 \\ \hline \end{array}$	$\begin{array}{r} 1 \\ \times 2 \\ \hline \end{array}$
4.	$\begin{array}{r} 2 \\ 2 \\ +2 \\ \hline \end{array}$	$\begin{array}{r} 2 \\ \times 3 \\ \hline \end{array}$	$\begin{array}{r} 3 \\ 3 \\ +3 \\ \hline \end{array}$	$\begin{array}{r} 3 \\ \times 3 \\ \hline \end{array}$	$\begin{array}{r} 4 \\ 4 \\ +4 \\ \hline \end{array}$	$\begin{array}{r} 4 \\ \times 3 \\ \hline \end{array}$
5.	$\begin{array}{r} 5 \\ 5 \\ +5 \\ \hline \end{array}$	$\begin{array}{r} 5 \\ \times 3 \\ \hline \end{array}$	$\begin{array}{r} 6 \\ 6 \\ +6 \\ \hline \end{array}$	$\begin{array}{r} 6 \\ \times 3 \\ \hline \end{array}$	$\begin{array}{r} 7 \\ 7 \\ +7 \\ \hline \end{array}$	$\begin{array}{r} 7 \\ \times 3 \\ \hline \end{array}$
6.	$\begin{array}{r} 8 \\ 8 \\ +8 \\ \hline \end{array}$	$\begin{array}{r} 8 \\ \times 3 \\ \hline \end{array}$	$\begin{array}{r} 9 \\ 9 \\ +9 \\ \hline \end{array}$	$\begin{array}{r} 9 \\ \times 3 \\ \hline \end{array}$	$\begin{array}{r} 1 \\ 1 \\ +1 \\ \hline \end{array}$	$\begin{array}{r} 1 \\ \times 3 \\ \hline \end{array}$

Lesson 3 Multiplication (by 0 and 1)

$$\begin{array}{r}1\\ \times0\\ \hline 0\end{array} \quad \begin{array}{r}2\\ \times0\\ \hline 0\end{array} \quad \begin{array}{r}0\\ \times3\\ \hline 0\end{array} \quad \begin{array}{r}0\\ \times4\\ \hline 0\end{array} \quad \Big| \quad \begin{array}{r}0\\ \times1\\ \hline 0\end{array} \quad \begin{array}{r}1\\ \times1\\ \hline 1\end{array} \quad \begin{array}{r}2\\ \times1\\ \hline 2\end{array} \quad \begin{array}{r}1\\ \times3\\ \hline 3\end{array}$$

Multiply.

	a	b	c	d	e	f
1.	$\begin{array}{r}0\\ \times2\\ \hline\end{array}$	$\begin{array}{r}9\\ \times1\\ \hline\end{array}$	$\begin{array}{r}1\\ \times7\\ \hline\end{array}$	$\begin{array}{r}6\\ \times0\\ \hline\end{array}$	$\begin{array}{r}1\\ \times5\\ \hline\end{array}$	$\begin{array}{r}0\\ \times7\\ \hline\end{array}$
2.	$\begin{array}{r}4\\ \times0\\ \hline\end{array}$	$\begin{array}{r}8\\ \times1\\ \hline\end{array}$	$\begin{array}{r}1\\ \times4\\ \hline\end{array}$	$\begin{array}{r}0\\ \times9\\ \hline\end{array}$	$\begin{array}{r}7\\ \times0\\ \hline\end{array}$	$\begin{array}{r}6\\ \times1\\ \hline\end{array}$
3.	$\begin{array}{r}5\\ \times0\\ \hline\end{array}$	$\begin{array}{r}0\\ \times8\\ \hline\end{array}$	$\begin{array}{r}5\\ \times1\\ \hline\end{array}$	$\begin{array}{r}1\\ \times6\\ \hline\end{array}$	$\begin{array}{r}1\\ \times1\\ \hline\end{array}$	$\begin{array}{r}8\\ \times0\\ \hline\end{array}$
4.	$\begin{array}{r}1\\ \times7\\ \hline\end{array}$	$\begin{array}{r}0\\ \times4\\ \hline\end{array}$	$\begin{array}{r}3\\ \times0\\ \hline\end{array}$	$\begin{array}{r}9\\ \times0\\ \hline\end{array}$	$\begin{array}{r}7\\ \times1\\ \hline\end{array}$	$\begin{array}{r}1\\ \times5\\ \hline\end{array}$
5.	$\begin{array}{r}0\\ \times7\\ \hline\end{array}$	$\begin{array}{r}1\\ \times9\\ \hline\end{array}$	$\begin{array}{r}1\\ \times6\\ \hline\end{array}$	$\begin{array}{r}0\\ \times5\\ \hline\end{array}$	$\begin{array}{r}1\\ \times0\\ \hline\end{array}$	$\begin{array}{r}2\\ \times1\\ \hline\end{array}$
6.	$\begin{array}{r}1\\ \times4\\ \hline\end{array}$	$\begin{array}{r}1\\ \times8\\ \hline\end{array}$	$\begin{array}{r}4\\ \times0\\ \hline\end{array}$	$\begin{array}{r}8\\ \times1\\ \hline\end{array}$	$\begin{array}{r}0\\ \times6\\ \hline\end{array}$	$\begin{array}{r}0\\ \times3\\ \hline\end{array}$
7.	$\begin{array}{r}0\\ \times9\\ \hline\end{array}$	$\begin{array}{r}6\\ \times1\\ \hline\end{array}$	$\begin{array}{r}0\\ \times2\\ \hline\end{array}$	$\begin{array}{r}9\\ \times1\\ \hline\end{array}$	$\begin{array}{r}0\\ \times1\\ \hline\end{array}$	$\begin{array}{r}3\\ \times1\\ \hline\end{array}$
8.	$\begin{array}{r}1\\ \times2\\ \hline\end{array}$	$\begin{array}{r}6\\ \times0\\ \hline\end{array}$	$\begin{array}{r}7\\ \times0\\ \hline\end{array}$	$\begin{array}{r}1\\ \times3\\ \hline\end{array}$	$\begin{array}{r}4\\ \times1\\ \hline\end{array}$	$\begin{array}{r}0\\ \times0\\ \hline\end{array}$

CHAPTER 8

Lesson 3 Problem Solving

BASEBALL CARDS - 9¢ each

FOOTBALL CARDS - 6¢ each

BASKETBALL CARDS - 5¢ each

Solve each problem.

1. Molly bought two baseball cards. Each baseball card cost 9 cents. How much did Molly pay for the baseball cards?

Molly bought _____ baseball cards.

Each baseball card cost _____ cents.

Molly paid _____ cents for the baseball cards.

1.

2. Cody bought two football cards. They cost 6 cents each. How much did Cody pay for the football cards?

Cody bought _____ football cards.

One football card cost _____ cents.

Cody paid _____ cents for the football cards.

2.

3. There are eight cards in each pack. How many cards are in three packs?

_____ cards are in three packs.

3.

4. One basketball card costs 5 cents. How much will eight basketball cards cost?

Eight basketball cards will cost _____ cents.

4.

Lesson 4 Multiplication (facts through 5 × 9)

6 ⟶ Find the **6**-row.

×4 ⟶ Find the **4**-column.

24 ⟵ The product is named where the 6-row and 4-column meet.

4-column

×	0	1	2	3	4	5	6	7	8	9
0	0	0	0	0	0	0	0	0	0	0
1	0	1	2	3	4	5	6	7	8	9
2	0	2	4	6	8	10	12	14	16	18
3	0	3	6	9	12	15	18	21	24	27
4	0	4	8	12	16	20	24	28	32	36
5	0	5	10	15	20	25	30	35	40	45
6	0	6	12	18	(24)	30				
7	0	7	14	21	28	35				
8	0	8	16	24	32	40				
9	0	9	18	27	36	45				

6-row --→

CHAPTER 8

Multiply.

	a	b	c	d	e	f
1.	5 ×4	8 ×4	7 ×5	6 ×5	2 ×4	4 ×3
2.	5 ×5	6 ×3	9 ×4	1 ×4	0 ×5	4 ×4
3.	3 ×5	7 ×4	2 ×5	4 ×2	8 ×5	9 ×2
4.	5 ×3	3 ×3	8 ×2	0 ×4	3 ×2	5 ×2
5.	6 ×4	8 ×3	4 ×1	5 ×0	5 ×1	6 ×2
6.	9 ×5	4 ×0	3 ×4	7 ×2	7 ×3	1 ×5

Lesson 4 Problem Solving

Solve each problem.

1. Ashley wants to buy five erasers. They cost 9 cents each. How much will she have to pay?

   Ashley wants to buy _____ erasers.

   One eraser costs _____ cents.

   Ashley will have to pay _____ cents.

2. There are five rows of mailboxes. There are seven mailboxes in each row. How many mailboxes are there in all?

   There are _____ mailboxes in each row.

   There are _____ rows of mailboxes.

   There are _____ mailboxes in all.

3. Milton, the pet monkey, eats four meals every day. How many meals does he eat in a week?

   There are _____ days in a week.

   Milton eats _____ meals every day.

   Milton eats _____ meals in a week.

4. In a baseball game each team gets three outs per inning. How many outs does each team get in a five-inning game?

   There are _____ innings in the game.

   Each team gets _____ outs per inning.

   Each team gets _____ outs in the five-inning game.

5. Cameron has gained 4 pounds in each of the past five months. How much weight has he gained?

   Cameron has gained _____ pounds in five months.

1.

2.

3.

4.

5.

Lesson 5 Multiplication Review

Multiply.

	a	*b*	*c*	*d*	*e*	*f*
1.	0 ×8	4 ×2	8 ×5	7 ×3	6 ×1	7 ×0
2.	1 ×1	9 ×2	4 ×4	3 ×5	6 ×5	1 ×4
3.	0 ×6	1 ×2	4 ×0	8 ×2	9 ×5	5 ×5
4.	8 ×4	6 ×3	1 ×5	9 ×0	2 ×1	7 ×2
5.	5 ×3	7 ×4	4 ×5	3 ×2	9 ×3	8 ×1
6.	6 ×0	3 ×1	6 ×2	0 ×0	2 ×3	9 ×4
7.	7 ×5	8 ×3	1 ×0	0 ×3	4 ×1	6 ×4
8.	5 ×4	2 ×2	9 ×1	1 ×7	2 ×4	3 ×3
9.	1 ×9	2 ×0	5 ×2	3 ×4	2 ×5	4 ×3

CHAPTER 8

Lesson 5   Problem Solving

Solve each problem.

1. Neal has six books. Each book weighs 1 kilogram. What is the weight of all the books?

   Neal has _____ books.

   Each book weighs _____ kilogram.

   The six books weigh _____ kilograms.

1.

2. A basketball game has four time periods. Kate's team is to play eight games. How many periods will her team play?

   Kate's team is to play _____ games.

   Each game has _____ time periods.

   Kate's team will play _____ time periods in all.

2.

3. Meagan works eight hours every day. How many hours does she work in five days?

   She works _____ hours in five days.

3.

4. Shane can ride his bicycle 5 miles in an hour. At that speed how far could he ride in two hours?

   Shane could ride _____ miles in two hours.

4.

5. Calvin bought five bags of balloons. Each bag had six balloons. How many balloons did he buy?

   Calvin bought _____ balloons in all.

5.

6. Kristen can build a model car in three hours. How long would it take her to build four model cars?

   Kristen could build four model cars in _____ hours.

6.

CHAPTER 8 PRACTICE TEST
Multiplication (basic facts through 5 × 9)

Multiply.

	a	b	c	d	e
1.	1 ×6	7 ×4	9 ×0	3 ×4	9 ×5
2.	4 ×3	7 ×3	0 ×6	1 ×4	6 ×2
3.	9 ×2	8 ×5	9 ×3	3 ×2	4 ×4
4.	0 ×1	5 ×5	9 ×4	3 ×0	4 ×5

Solve each problem.

5. Nathan bought five boxes of pencils. There are six pencils in each box. How many pencils did he buy?

Nathan bought _____ boxes of pencils.

There are _____ pencils in each box.

He bought _____ pencils in all.

6. Erin is to put four apples in each bag. How many apples does she need to fill eight bags?

Erin needs _____ apples in all.

7. Troy bought three boxes of crayons. Each box held eight crayons. How many crayons did he buy?

Troy bought _____ crayons.

5.

6.

7.

CHAPTER 9 PRETEST
Multiplication (basic facts through 9 × 9)

Multiply.

	a	*b*	*c*	*d*	*e*	*f*
1.	7 ×6	6 ×6	4 ×6	8 ×6	5 ×6	9 ×6
2.	8 ×7	4 ×7	9 ×7	7 ×7	6 ×7	5 ×7
3.	9 ×8	5 ×8	7 ×8	8 ×8	6 ×8	4 ×8
4.	6 ×9	9 ×9	5 ×9	8 ×9	4 ×9	7 ×9

Solve each problem.

5. Luke set up nine rows of chairs. He put nine chairs in each row. How many chairs did he use?

Luke used _____ chairs.

6. Bethany's dad works eight hours every day. How many hours would he work in seven days?

He would work _____ hours in seven days.

7. There are nine players on a team. How many players are there on seven teams?

There are _____ players on seven teams.

8. Brent puts six apples into each bag. How many apples would he need to fill seven bags?

He would need _____ apples.

5.

6.

7.

8.

Lesson 1 Multiplication (facts through 6 × 9)

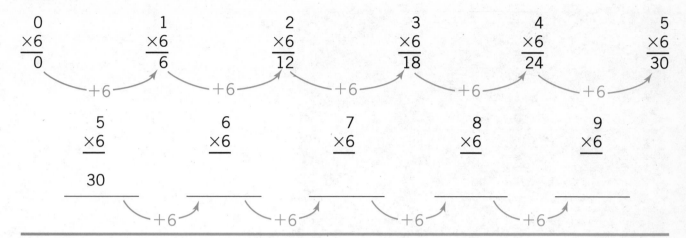

Multiply.

	a	b	c	d	e	f
1.	5 ×6	3 ×3	9 ×6	8 ×4	0 ×5	5 ×3
2.	8 ×5	2 ×6	6 ×4	5 ×5	3 ×4	6 ×1
3.	4 ×3	7 ×4	6 ×5	8 ×6	9 ×4	8 ×3
4.	0 ×3	3 ×6	1 ×5	4 ×4	2 ×3	4 ×5
5.	7 ×6	9 ×5	7 ×5	0 ×4	5 ×2	2 ×4
6.	6 ×6	6 ×2	5 ×4	1 ×3	3 ×5	0 ×6
7.	1 ×4	2 ×5	1 ×6	9 ×3	7 ×3	4 ×6

Lesson 1 Problem Solving

Solve each problem.

1. There are six rows of cactus plants. Each row has four plants. How many cactus plants are there in all?

    There are _____ rows of cactus plants.

    There are _____ cactus plants in each row.

    There are _____ cactus plants in all.

1.

2. There are eight marigold plants in each row. There are six rows. How many marigold plants are there?

    There are _____ marigold plants in each row.

    There are _____ rows of marigold plants.

    There are _____ marigold plants in all.

2.

3. There are six rosebushes in each row. There are nine rows. How many rosebushes are there?

    There are _____ rosebushes in each row.

    There are _____ rows of rosebushes.

    There are _____ rosebushes in all.

3.

Lesson 2 Multiplication (facts through 8 × 9)

$$\begin{array}{cccccc}
4 & 5 & 6 & 7 & 8 & 9 \\
\times 7 & \times 7 & \times 7 & \times 7 & \times 7 & \times 7 \\
\hline
28 & 35 & 42 \\
\end{array}$$

+7 +7 +7 +7 +7

$$\begin{array}{cccccc}
4 & 5 & 6 & 7 & 8 & 9 \\
\times 8 & \times 8 & \times 8 & \times 8 & \times 8 & \times 8 \\
\hline
32 & 40 & 48 \\
\end{array}$$

+8 +8 +8 +8 +8

Multiply.

	a	b	c	d	e	f
1.	7 ×7	7 ×6	6 ×8	3 ×7	9 ×8	0 ×7
2.	8 ×8	8 ×5	1 ×8	7 ×3	3 ×8	1 ×7
3.	8 ×0	8 ×6	5 ×8	9 ×7	7 ×1	6 ×7
4.	7 ×8	5 ×7	7 ×0	7 ×2	7 ×5	0 ×8
5.	8 ×7	2 ×8	8 ×4	7 ×4	8 ×3	4 ×8
6.	9 ×4	8 ×1	4 ×7	8 ×2	2 ×7	9 ×6

Lesson 2 Problem Solving

Solve each problem.

1. In Tori's building there are seven floors. There are nine apartments on each floor. How many apartments are in the building?

   There are _____ floors in this building.

   There are _____ apartments on each floor.

   There are _____ apartments in this building.

2. The science club meets four times each month. The club meets for seven months. How many meetings will the science club have?

   The science club meets _____ times each month.

   The club meets for _____ months.

   The club will have _____ meetings in all.

3. Each bag of corn weighs 8 kilograms. There are seven bags. How much do the bags weigh in all?

   Each bag weighs _____ kilograms.

   There are _____ bags.

   The bags weigh _____ kilograms in all.

4. There are seven days in a week. How many days are there in five weeks?

   There are _____ days in five weeks.

5. Brenda walks six blocks each day going to and from school. How many blocks does she walk going to and from school in seven days?

   Brenda walks _____ blocks in seven days.

1.
2.
3.

4.	5.

CHAPTER 9
Multiplication (basic facts through 9 × 9)

Lesson 2
Multiplication (facts through 8 × 9)

124

Lesson 3 Multiplication (facts through 9 × 9)

9-column

×	0	1	2	3	4	5	6	7	8	9
0	0	0	0	0	0	0	0	0	0	0
1	0	1	2	3	4	5	6	7	8	9
2	0	2	4	6	8	10	12	14	16	18
3	0	3	6	9	12	15	18	21	24	27
4	0	4	8	12	16	20	24	28	32	36
5	0	5	10	15	20	25	30	35	40	45
6	0	6	12	18	24	30	36	42	48	54
7	0	7	14	21	28	35	42	49	56	63
8	0	8	16	24	32	40	48	56	64	72
9	0	9	18	27	36	45	54	63	72	81

$$9 \longrightarrow \text{Find the } \boxed{9}\text{-row.}$$
$$\underline{\times 9} \longrightarrow \text{Find the } \boxed{9}\text{-column.}$$
$$81 \longleftarrow \text{The product is named where the 9-row and 9-column meet.}$$

9-row

CHAPTER 9

Multiply.

	a	b	c	d	e	f
1.	7 ×9	9 ×6	8 ×8	3 ×7	2 ×9	7 ×3
2.	8 ×5	8 ×7	4 ×9	6 ×8	7 ×0	7 ×7
3.	9 ×9	1 ×8	0 ×9	6 ×9	7 ×8	2 ×8
4.	4 ×8	0 ×7	4 ×7	9 ×2	8 ×4	6 ×7
5.	5 ×8	9 ×7	3 ×8	1 ×9	1 ×7	0 ×8
6.	5 ×9	8 ×0	3 ×9	5 ×7	8 ×9	2 ×7

Lesson 3 Problem Solving

Solve each problem.

1. There are eight chairs around each table. There are nine tables. How many chairs are around all the tables?

There are _____ chairs around each table.

There are _____ tables.

There are _____ chairs around all the tables.

2. Workers are eating lunch at nine tables. Each table has nine workers. How many workers are eating lunch?

There are _____ tables.

_____ workers are at each table.

_____ workers are eating lunch.

3. The group of workers drinks 9 liters of milk each day. They are at work five days each week. How many liters of milk do they drink in five days?

They drink _____ liters of milk in five days.

4. A bowling league bowls four times each month. How many times will the league bowl in nine months?

The bowling league will bowl _____ times.

5. There are nine packages of golf balls. Each package has six golf balls. How many golf balls are there in all?

There are _____ golf balls.

6. A regular baseball game is nine innings long. How many innings are in seven regular games?

There are _____ innings in seven regular games.

1.	
2.	
3.	4.
5.	6.

Lesson 4 Multiplication Review

Multiply.

	a	b	c	d	e	f
1.	7 ×9	6 ×7	1 ×5	2 ×9	3 ×6	8 ×8
2.	3 ×7	4 ×9	0 ×8	7 ×5	7 ×8	6 ×6
3.	9 ×5	4 ×6	5 ×9	2 ×8	8 ×7	0 ×7
4.	7 ×6	1 ×6	9 ×8	0 ×9	5 ×5	9 ×7
5.	8 ×5	4 ×8	4 ×7	0 ×6	1 ×9	4 ×5
6.	6 ×8	9 ×6	6 ×5	6 ×4	7 ×7	3 ×9
7.	8 ×6	5 ×8	7 ×4	3 ×5	9 ×9	1 ×7
8.	9 ×4	5 ×7	1 ×8	8 ×9	5 ×6	2 ×5
9.	2 ×6	0 ×5	6 ×9	3 ×8	8 ×4	2 ×7

Lesson 4 Problem Solving

Solve each problem.

1. Some students formed five teams. There were eight students on each team. How many students were there?

   There were _____ teams.

   There were _____ students on each team.

   There were _____ students in all.

2. The waiter put nine napkins on each table. There were nine tables. How many napkins did the waiter use?

   The waiter put _____ napkins on each table.

   There were _____ tables.

   The waiter used _____ napkins in all.

3. Dr. Mede rides her bicycle 6 kilometers every day. How far would she ride in nine days?

   Dr. Mede rides _____ kilometers every day.

   She rides for each of _____ days.

   She would ride _____ kilometers in all.

4. Mr. Brown works seven hours each day. How many hours will he work in six days?

   Mr. Brown will work _____ hours in six days.

5. There are eight hot dogs in each package. How many hot dogs are there in nine packages?

   There are _____ hot dogs in nine packages.

6. Suppose you read eight stories every day. How many stories would you read in seven days?

   You would read _____ stories in seven days.

1.	
2.	
3.	4.
5.	6.

CHAPTER 9 PRACTICE TEST
Multiplication (basic facts through 9 × 9)

Multiply.

	a	*b*	*c*	*d*	*e*
1.	6 ×7	5 ×9	8 ×6	4 ×7	7 ×7
2.	9 ×7	9 ×9	1 ×7	4 ×6	7 ×9
3.	0 ×6	7 ×8	5 ×8	9 ×8	7 ×6
4.	8 ×9	4 ×8	9 ×6	2 ×7	3 ×9

Solve each problem.

5. A clerk puts six oranges in each package. How many oranges are needed to make nine packages?

There are _____ oranges in each package.

There are to be _____ packages.

_____ oranges are needed in all.

5.

6. A barbershop can handle eight customers in one hour. How many customers can it handle in eight hours?

It can handle _____ customers.

6.

7. Mr. Lawkin put three pictures in a row. He made eight rows. How many pictures did he use?

Mr. Lawkin used _____ pictures.

7.

CHAPTER 10 PRETEST
Multiplication (2-digit by 1-digit)

Multiply.

	a	*b*	*c*	*d*	*e*	*f*
1.	3 ×2	3 0 ×2	2 ×4	2 0 ×4	1 ×7	1 0 ×7
2.	3 2 ×3	2 4 ×2	1 3 ×3	2 1 ×4	1 1 ×5	2 3 ×3
3.	7 ×4	7 0 ×4	6 ×3	6 0 ×3	9 ×4	9 0 ×4
4.	6 2 ×3	7 4 ×2	3 1 ×8	6 2 ×4	8 3 ×2	4 1 ×5
5.	1 8 ×4	2 6 ×3	3 5 ×2	2 4 ×3	3 8 ×2	1 6 ×5
6.	4 3 ×4	2 7 ×5	3 5 ×3	4 6 ×6	2 8 ×6	5 4 ×5
7.	5 6 ×7	6 3 ×2	8 0 ×5	2 3 ×2	3 7 ×2	4 5 ×5
8.	1 7 ×4	4 0 ×8	7 3 ×3	2 2 ×3	5 4 ×3	2 7 ×6
9.	3 0 ×9	5 8 ×4	2 8 ×4	2 5 ×3	8 0 ×4	6 6 ×2

Lesson 1　Multiplication (by tens)

$$\begin{array}{r} 4 \\ \times 2 \\ \hline 8 \end{array} \quad \begin{array}{r} 40 \\ \times 2 \\ \hline 80 \end{array} \quad \begin{array}{r} 2 \\ \times 3 \\ \hline 6 \end{array} \quad \begin{array}{r} 20 \\ \times 3 \\ \hline 60 \end{array} \quad \Big| \quad \begin{array}{r} 7 \\ \times 3 \\ \hline 21 \end{array} \quad \begin{array}{r} 70 \\ \times 3 \\ \hline 210 \end{array} \quad \begin{array}{r} 8 \\ \times 4 \\ \hline 32 \end{array} \quad \begin{array}{r} 80 \\ \times 4 \\ \hline 320 \end{array}$$

Multiply.

	a	b	c	d	e	f
1.	$\begin{array}{r}3\\\times2\\\hline\end{array}$	$\begin{array}{r}30\\\times2\\\hline\end{array}$	$\begin{array}{r}2\\\times4\\\hline\end{array}$	$\begin{array}{r}20\\\times4\\\hline\end{array}$	$\begin{array}{r}6\\\times1\\\hline\end{array}$	$\begin{array}{r}60\\\times1\\\hline\end{array}$
2.	$\begin{array}{r}10\\\times8\\\hline\end{array}$	$\begin{array}{r}40\\\times2\\\hline\end{array}$	$\begin{array}{r}10\\\times9\\\hline\end{array}$	$\begin{array}{r}10\\\times3\\\hline\end{array}$	$\begin{array}{r}30\\\times3\\\hline\end{array}$	$\begin{array}{r}70\\\times1\\\hline\end{array}$
3.	$\begin{array}{r}9\\\times4\\\hline\end{array}$	$\begin{array}{r}90\\\times4\\\hline\end{array}$	$\begin{array}{r}6\\\times3\\\hline\end{array}$	$\begin{array}{r}60\\\times3\\\hline\end{array}$	$\begin{array}{r}5\\\times5\\\hline\end{array}$	$\begin{array}{r}50\\\times5\\\hline\end{array}$
4.	$\begin{array}{r}70\\\times3\\\hline\end{array}$	$\begin{array}{r}60\\\times5\\\hline\end{array}$	$\begin{array}{r}40\\\times4\\\hline\end{array}$	$\begin{array}{r}50\\\times2\\\hline\end{array}$	$\begin{array}{r}80\\\times3\\\hline\end{array}$	$\begin{array}{r}90\\\times6\\\hline\end{array}$
5.	$\begin{array}{r}20\\\times4\\\hline\end{array}$	$\begin{array}{r}30\\\times5\\\hline\end{array}$	$\begin{array}{r}40\\\times3\\\hline\end{array}$	$\begin{array}{r}20\\\times2\\\hline\end{array}$	$\begin{array}{r}30\\\times6\\\hline\end{array}$	$\begin{array}{r}40\\\times7\\\hline\end{array}$
6.	$\begin{array}{r}70\\\times7\\\hline\end{array}$	$\begin{array}{r}30\\\times8\\\hline\end{array}$	$\begin{array}{r}10\\\times7\\\hline\end{array}$	$\begin{array}{r}80\\\times8\\\hline\end{array}$	$\begin{array}{r}90\\\times1\\\hline\end{array}$	$\begin{array}{r}60\\\times4\\\hline\end{array}$
7.	$\begin{array}{r}40\\\times5\\\hline\end{array}$	$\begin{array}{r}20\\\times8\\\hline\end{array}$	$\begin{array}{r}60\\\times2\\\hline\end{array}$	$\begin{array}{r}50\\\times3\\\hline\end{array}$	$\begin{array}{r}10\\\times5\\\hline\end{array}$	$\begin{array}{r}40\\\times1\\\hline\end{array}$
8.	$\begin{array}{r}60\\\times7\\\hline\end{array}$	$\begin{array}{r}50\\\times5\\\hline\end{array}$	$\begin{array}{r}80\\\times3\\\hline\end{array}$	$\begin{array}{r}20\\\times9\\\hline\end{array}$	$\begin{array}{r}70\\\times8\\\hline\end{array}$	$\begin{array}{r}90\\\times3\\\hline\end{array}$

CHAPTER 10

Lesson 1   Problem Solving

Solve each problem.

1. There are four classrooms on the first floor. Each classroom has 30 seats. How many seats are on the first floor?

   _____ seats are in each classroom.

   _____ classrooms are on the first floor.

   _____ seats are on the first floor.

2. Laura placed two boxes on a wagon. Each box weighs 20 kilograms. How much do the two boxes weigh?

   Each box weighs _____ kilograms.

   Laura placed _____ boxes on the wagon.

   The two boxes weigh _____ kilograms.

3. Trent bought three packages of paper. Each package had 30 sheets. How many sheets of paper did he buy?

   Each package contains _____ sheets of paper.

   Trent bought _____ packages of paper.

   Trent bought _____ sheets of paper.

4. Mrs. Long bought six boxes of nails. Each box had 30 nails. How many nails did she buy?

   Mrs. Long bought _____ nails.

5. There are 40 bottles in a case. How many bottles are there in two cases?

   There are _____ bottles in two cases.

6. A bus has 40 passenger seats. How many passenger seats are there on seven such buses?

   There are _____ passenger seats on seven buses.

1.

2.

3.   4.

5.   6.

Lesson 2 Multiplication (2-digit by 1-digit)

	Multiply 2 ones by 3.	Multiply 7 tens by 3.	
72 ×3	72 ×3 6	72 ×3 6 210	72 ×3 6 210 } Add. 216

Multiply.

	a	*b*	*c*	*d*	*e*	*f*
1.	6 2 ×2	7 3 ×3	9 2 ×4	8 4 ×2	5 3 ×2	4 2 ×3
2.	2 3 ×2	3 1 ×3	4 2 ×2	1 2 ×4	3 3 ×3	4 2 ×2
3.	2 1 ×4	6 1 ×3	5 1 ×2	4 3 ×2	8 2 ×4	1 3 ×3
4.	7 2 ×3	3 2 ×3	4 3 ×3	2 3 ×3	3 4 ×2	9 3 ×2

CHAPTER 10

Lesson 3 Multiplication (2-digit by 1-digit)

Multiply
4 ones by 2.

Multiply.
8 tens by 2.

$$\begin{array}{r} 84 \\ \times 2 \\ \hline \end{array}$$

$$\begin{array}{r} 84 \\ \times 2 \\ \hline 8 \end{array}$$

$$\begin{array}{r} 84 \\ \times 2 \\ \hline 168 \end{array}$$

Multiply.

	a	b	c	d	e	f
1.	6 2 ×4	8 4 ×2	7 3 ×3	8 2 ×2	9 1 ×2	5 2 ×3
2.	4 3 ×2	4 1 ×4	3 2 ×3	6 1 ×3	4 2 ×4	4 4 ×2
3.	7 2 ×3	7 1 ×3	8 1 ×2	4 3 ×3	5 2 ×4	8 3 ×2
4.	6 2 ×2	9 3 ×3	5 2 ×1	7 4 ×2	5 3 ×2	6 2 ×3
5.	7 2 ×4	8 1 ×5	9 2 ×3	6 3 ×3	5 4 ×2	7 3 ×2
6.	6 1 ×7	3 2 ×4	8 2 ×3	8 1 ×9	6 3 ×2	9 1 ×5
7.	5 3 ×3	7 1 ×6	8 2 ×4	9 1 ×9	9 2 ×4	8 1 ×8

Lesson 4 Multiplication (with renaming)

Multiply
7 ones by 3.

Multiply 1 ten by 3.
Add the 2 tens.

$$
\begin{array}{r} 17 \\ \times 3 \\ \hline \end{array}
\qquad
\begin{array}{r} ^2 \\ 17 \\ \times 3 \\ \hline 1 \end{array}
\qquad
\begin{array}{r} ^2 \\ 17 \\ \times 3 \\ \hline 51 \end{array}
\qquad
\begin{array}{r} 17 \\ \times 3 \\ \hline 51 \end{array}
$$

$$3 \times 7 = 21 = 20 + 1 \qquad 3 \times 10 = 30$$
$$30 + 20 = 50$$

Multiply.

	a	b	c	d	e	f
1.	$\begin{array}{r}23\\ \times 4\\\hline\end{array}$	$\begin{array}{r}29\\ \times 3\\\hline\end{array}$	$\begin{array}{r}16\\ \times 5\\\hline\end{array}$	$\begin{array}{r}14\\ \times 7\\\hline\end{array}$	$\begin{array}{r}26\\ \times 3\\\hline\end{array}$	$\begin{array}{r}12\\ \times 8\\\hline\end{array}$
2.	$\begin{array}{r}37\\ \times 2\\\hline\end{array}$	$\begin{array}{r}26\\ \times 2\\\hline\end{array}$	$\begin{array}{r}47\\ \times 2\\\hline\end{array}$	$\begin{array}{r}28\\ \times 3\\\hline\end{array}$	$\begin{array}{r}15\\ \times 5\\\hline\end{array}$	$\begin{array}{r}24\\ \times 4\\\hline\end{array}$
3.	$\begin{array}{r}18\\ \times 5\\\hline\end{array}$	$\begin{array}{r}14\\ \times 5\\\hline\end{array}$	$\begin{array}{r}28\\ \times 3\\\hline\end{array}$	$\begin{array}{r}35\\ \times 2\\\hline\end{array}$	$\begin{array}{r}46\\ \times 2\\\hline\end{array}$	$\begin{array}{r}38\\ \times 2\\\hline\end{array}$
4.	$\begin{array}{r}45\\ \times 2\\\hline\end{array}$	$\begin{array}{r}27\\ \times 3\\\hline\end{array}$	$\begin{array}{r}15\\ \times 6\\\hline\end{array}$	$\begin{array}{r}12\\ \times 7\\\hline\end{array}$	$\begin{array}{r}15\\ \times 4\\\hline\end{array}$	$\begin{array}{r}48\\ \times 2\\\hline\end{array}$
5.	$\begin{array}{r}28\\ \times 2\\\hline\end{array}$	$\begin{array}{r}12\\ \times 6\\\hline\end{array}$	$\begin{array}{r}17\\ \times 5\\\hline\end{array}$	$\begin{array}{r}13\\ \times 6\\\hline\end{array}$	$\begin{array}{r}19\\ \times 3\\\hline\end{array}$	$\begin{array}{r}19\\ \times 4\\\hline\end{array}$
6.	$\begin{array}{r}36\\ \times 2\\\hline\end{array}$	$\begin{array}{r}24\\ \times 3\\\hline\end{array}$	$\begin{array}{r}25\\ \times 3\\\hline\end{array}$	$\begin{array}{r}16\\ \times 4\\\hline\end{array}$	$\begin{array}{r}29\\ \times 2\\\hline\end{array}$	$\begin{array}{r}18\\ \times 3\\\hline\end{array}$

CHAPTER 10

Lesson 4 Problem Solving

Solve each problem.

1. Ms. McClean ordered 7 dozen radio antennas. How
   many antennas did she order? (There are 12 items
   in a dozen.)

   There are _____ items in a dozen.

   She ordered _____ dozen antennas.

   Ms. McClean ordered _____ radio antennas.

2. There are 14 CD players on a shelf. Each player
   weighs 5 kilograms. How much do all the players
   weigh?

   There are _____ CD players.

   Each player weighs _____ kilograms.

   All the players weigh _____ kilograms.

3. Mr. Tunin bought two CD players. Each player cost
   $49. How much did both players cost?

   Both players cost $ _____.

4. Ms. McClean sold 36 radios this week. She sold the
   same number of radios last week. How many
   radios did she sell in the two weeks?

   She sold _____ radios in the two weeks.

1.	
2.	
3.	4.

Lesson 5 Multiplication (with renaming)

Multiply
7 ones by 5.

Multiply 5 tens by 5.
Add the 3 tens.

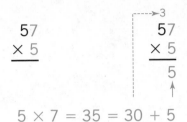

$$57 \times 5$$

$$5 \times 7 = 35 = 30 + 5$$

$$5 \times 50 = 250$$

$$57 \times 5 \over 285$$

$$250 + 30 = 280 = 200 + 80$$

Multiply.

	a	b	c	d	e	f
1.	3 5 ×4	4 2 ×6	5 6 ×3	4 7 ×5	3 8 ×6	2 5 ×5
2.	5 4 ×4	2 7 ×6	3 8 ×5	4 8 ×8	8 3 ×7	7 4 ×6
3.	7 5 ×4	5 8 ×3	4 6 ×4	3 7 ×6	2 9 ×5	4 6 ×3
4.	8 4 ×4	9 3 ×6	6 2 ×8	5 7 ×5	3 9 ×4	2 2 ×7
5.	4 5 ×6	6 8 ×7	7 3 ×9	8 7 ×8	9 4 ×6	8 3 ×4
6.	9 6 ×5	8 5 ×3	4 7 ×4	2 3 ×9	3 9 ×7	6 5 ×6

CHAPTER 10

Lesson 5 Problem Solving

Solve each problem.

1. Jordan's spelling book has 25 new words on each page. There are nine pages in the first section. How many new words are there in the first section?

   There are _____ new spelling words on each page.

   There are _____ pages in the first section.

   There are _____ new spelling words in the first section.

2. Alan wants to walk up six flights of stairs. There are 26 steps in each flight. How many steps will he have to walk up?

   There are _____ steps in each flight.

   Alan wants to walk up _____ flights.

   Alan will have to walk up _____ steps.

3. There are seven rows of seats in the balcony. There are 36 seats in each row. How many seats are in the balcony?

   There are _____ seats in each row.

   There are _____ rows.

   There are _____ seats in the balcony.

4. There are 25 baseball players on each team. How many players are there on eight such teams?

   There are _____ players on eight teams.

5. Brenna used three rolls of film. She took 36 pictures on each roll. How many pictures did Brenna take?

   Brenna took _____ pictures.

1.

2.

3.

4.   5.

CHAPTER 10 PRACTICE TEST
Multiplication (2-digit by 1-digit)

Multiply.

	a	b	c	d	e
1.	3 0 ×2	4 2 ×2	2 3 ×3	6 0 ×4	8 0 ×3
2.	8 4 ×2	7 3 ×3	2 1 ×7	1 4 ×6	2 7 ×3
3.	5 7 ×5	3 8 ×6	4 2 ×5	2 9 ×4	3 6 ×5
4.	1 5 ×4	7 3 ×2	5 8 ×3	4 0 ×9	2 8 ×3

Solve each problem.

5. Morgan has four decks of cards. There are 52 cards in each deck. How many cards does she have?

5.

She has _____ decks.

There are _____ cards in each deck.

Morgan has _____ cards in all.

6. Blake's father works 37 hours each week. How many hours would he work in four weeks?

6.　　　　**7.**

He would work _____ hours in four weeks.

7. Mr. Richards gave each student three sheets of paper. There were 28 students. How many sheets of paper did he use?

Mr. Richards used _____ sheets of paper.

CHAPTER 11 PRETEST
Division (basic facts through 45 ÷ 5)

Divide.

	a	b	c	d	e
1.	2)‾6	2)‾1 2	2)‾1 8	2)‾4	2)‾1 0
2.	4)‾1 6	3)‾2 4	3)‾9	5)‾2 5	3)‾3
3.	1)‾4	1)‾8	1)‾1 6	4)‾3 6	1)‾2 7
4.	2)‾1 6	1)‾1	3)‾2 7	1)‾6	1)‾2 1
5.	1)‾1 2	5)‾2 0	2)‾1 4	4)‾8	1)‾1 4
6.	1)‾5	4)‾2 8	5)‾5	1)‾2	3)‾1 8

Solve each problem.

7. Paula has 18 books. She put them in piles of 3 books each. How many piles of books does she have?

She has _____ piles of books.

7.

8. Bart has 12 pennies. He put 3 pennies in each stack. How many stacks of pennies does he have?

He has _____ stacks of pennies.

8.

9. Dee has 12 pennies. She put 2 pennies in each stack. How many stacks of pennies does she have?

She has _____ stacks of pennies.

9.

Lesson 1 Division (introduction)

÷ and $\overline{)}$ mean divide.

6 ÷ 2 = 3 is read "6 divided by 2 is equal to 3."

8 ÷ 2 = 4 is read "_____ divided by 2 is equal to _____."

$2\overline{)6}$ with quotient 3 is read "6 divided by 2 is equal to 3."

$2\overline{)8}$ with quotient 4 is read "_____ divided by 2 is equal to _____."

divisor ------→ $2\overline{)6}$ ←------- dividend, with 3 ←------- quotient

In $2\overline{)8}$ with 4, the divisor is _____, the dividend is _____, and the quotient is _____.

Complete each sentence.

1. 10 ÷ 2 = 5 is read "_____ divided by 2 is equal to _____."

2. 21 ÷ 3 = 7 is read "_____ divided by 3 is equal to _____."

3. 4 ÷ 2 = 2 is read "_____ divided by 2 is equal to _____."

4. $3\overline{)18}$ with 6 is read "_____ divided by 3 is equal to _____."

5. $2\overline{)18}$ with 9 is read "_____ divided by 2 is equal to _____."

6. $3\overline{)24}$ with 8 is read "_____ divided by 3 is equal to _____."

7. In $3\overline{)21}$ with 7, the divisor is _____, the dividend is _____, and the quotient is _____.

8. In $2\overline{)4}$ with 2, the divisor is _____, the dividend is _____, and the quotient is _____.

9. In $2\overline{)10}$ with 5, the divisor is _____, the dividend is _____, and the quotient is _____.

10. In $3\overline{)18}$ with 6, the divisor is _____, the dividend is _____, and the quotient is _____.

Lesson 2 Division (concept)

6 ✕s in all.
2 ✕s in each group.

How many groups?

6 ÷ 2 = ___3___

There are ___3___ groups.

6 ✕s in all.
3 groups of ✕s.

How many ✕s in each group?

6 ÷ 3 = _____

There are _____ ✕s in each group.

Complete the following.

	a		*b*

1. 10 ☆s in all.
  2 ☆s in each group.

  How many groups?

10 ÷ 2 = _____

There are _____ groups.

10 ☆s in all.
5 groups of ☆s.

How many ☆s in each group?

10 ÷ 5 = _____

There are _____ ☆s in each group.

2. 8 ◻s in all.

  _____ ◻s in each group.
  How many groups?

8 ÷ 2 = _____

There are _____ groups.

_____ ◻s in all.

4 groups of ◻s.
How many ◻s in each group?

8 ÷ 4 = _____

There are _____ ◻s in each group.

3. _____ ◯s in all.

  _____ ◯s in each group.
  How many groups?

4 ÷ 2 = _____

There are _____ groups.

_____ ◯s in all.

_____ groups of ◯s.
How many ◯s in each group?

4 ÷ 2 = _____

There are _____ ◯s in each group.

Lesson 3   Division (facts through 27 ÷ 3)

$$
\begin{array}{r} 3 \\ \times 2 \\ \hline 6 \end{array}
\;\dashrightarrow\;
2\overline{)6}\;\;3
$$

$$
\begin{array}{r} 4 \\ \times 3 \\ \hline 12 \end{array}
\;\dashrightarrow\;
3\overline{)12}\;\;4
$$

If 2 × 3 = 6, then 6 ÷ 2 = 3.   If 3 × 4 = 12, then _____ ÷ 3 = _____.

Divide as shown.

	a		*b*	

1.
$\begin{array}{r} 5 \\ \times 2 \\ \hline 10 \end{array}$
$2\overline{)10}\;\;5$
$\begin{array}{r} 6 \\ \times 3 \\ \hline 18 \end{array}$
$3\overline{)18}$

2.
$\begin{array}{r} 7 \\ \times 2 \\ \hline 14 \end{array}$
$2\overline{)14}$
$\begin{array}{r} 8 \\ \times 3 \\ \hline 24 \end{array}$
$3\overline{)24}$

3.
$\begin{array}{r} 1 \\ \times 2 \\ \hline 2 \end{array}$
$2\overline{)2}$
$\begin{array}{r} 3 \\ \times 3 \\ \hline 9 \end{array}$
$3\overline{)9}$

4.
$\begin{array}{r} 8 \\ \times 2 \\ \hline 16 \end{array}$
$2\overline{)16}$
$\begin{array}{r} 9 \\ \times 3 \\ \hline 27 \end{array}$
$3\overline{)27}$

Divide.

	a	*b*	*c*	*d*
5.	$3\overline{)15}$	$2\overline{)6}$	$3\overline{)3}$	$3\overline{)6}$
6.	$3\overline{)21}$	$2\overline{)18}$	$2\overline{)8}$	$2\overline{)12}$

CHAPTER 11

Lesson 3   Problem Solving

Solve each problem.

1. Twenty-four people are at work. They work in three departments. The same number of people work in each department. How many people work in each department?

   There are _____ people.

   They work in _____ departments.

   There are _____ people in each department.

2. Dan put eight books into two stacks. Each stack had the same number of books. How many books were in each stack?

   There were _____ books in all.

   They were put into _____ stacks.

   There were _____ books in each stack.

3. Janice put 16 liters of water into two jars. She put the same number of liters into each jar. How many liters of water did she put into each jar?

   Janice put _____ liters of water into jars.

   She used _____ jars.

   Janice put _____ liters of water into each jar.

4. Kim has 27 apples. She wants to put the same number of apples in each of three boxes. How many apples should she put in each box?

   She should put _____ apples in each box.

5. Mr. Green had 18 inches of wire. He cut the wire into two pieces. The pieces were the same length. How long was each piece?

   Each piece was _____ inches long.

1.

2.

3.

4.

5.

Lesson 4   Division (facts through 45 ÷ 5)

$$
\begin{array}{r} 5 \\ \times 4 \\ \hline 20 \end{array}
\quad\longrightarrow\quad
\begin{array}{r} 5 \\ 4\overline{)\,20} \end{array}
\qquad\qquad
\begin{array}{r} 9 \\ \times 5 \\ \hline 45 \end{array}
\quad\longrightarrow\quad
\begin{array}{r} 9 \\ 5\overline{)\,45} \end{array}
$$

If 4 × 5 = 20, then 20 ÷ 4 = 5.   If 5 × 9 = 45, then _____ ÷ 5 = _____.

Divide as shown.

	a		*b*	

1.
$$\begin{array}{r} 7 \\ \times 4 \\ \hline 28 \end{array} \qquad 4\overline{)\,2\,8} \qquad\qquad \begin{array}{r} 6 \\ \times 5 \\ \hline 30 \end{array} \qquad 5\overline{)\,3\,0}$$

2.
$$\begin{array}{r} 4 \\ \times 4 \\ \hline 16 \end{array} \qquad 4\overline{)\,1\,6} \qquad\qquad \begin{array}{r} 3 \\ \times 5 \\ \hline 15 \end{array} \qquad 5\overline{)\,1\,5}$$

3.
$$\begin{array}{r} 6 \\ \times 4 \\ \hline 24 \end{array} \qquad 4\overline{)\,2\,4} \qquad\qquad \begin{array}{r} 4 \\ \times 5 \\ \hline 20 \end{array} \qquad 5\overline{)\,2\,0}$$

4.
$$\begin{array}{r} 9 \\ \times 4 \\ \hline 36 \end{array} \qquad 4\overline{)\,3\,6} \qquad\qquad \begin{array}{r} 8 \\ \times 5 \\ \hline 40 \end{array} \qquad 5\overline{)\,4\,0}$$

Divide.

a	*b*	*c*	*d*

5. $4\overline{)\,8}$ $\qquad\qquad$ $5\overline{)\,1\,0}$ $\qquad\qquad$ $4\overline{)\,4}$ $\qquad\qquad$ $4\overline{)\,1\,2}$

6. $5\overline{)\,2\,5}$ $\qquad\qquad$ $5\overline{)\,5}$ $\qquad\qquad$ $4\overline{)\,3\,2}$ $\qquad\qquad$ $5\overline{)\,3\,5}$

Lesson 4 Problem Solving

Solve each problem.

1. A loaf of bread has 24 slices. Mrs. Spencer uses 4 slices each day. How long will a loaf of bread last her?

   A loaf of bread has _____ slices.

   Mrs. Spencer uses _____ slices a day.

   The loaf of bread will last _____ days.

2. A football team played 28 periods. There are 4 periods in a game. How many games did they play?

   The football team played _____ periods.

   There are _____ periods each game.

   The football team played _____ games.

3. A basketball game is 32 minutes long. The game is separated into four parts. Each part has the same number of minutes. How long is each part?

   A basketball game is _____ minutes long.

   The game is separated into _____ parts.

   Each part is _____ minutes long.

4. Emma worked 25 problems. She worked 5 problems on each sheet of paper. How many sheets of paper did she use?

   She used _____ sheets of paper.

5. Robert works the same number of hours each week. He worked 45 hours in five weeks. How many hours does he work each week?

   Robert works _____ hours each week.

1.

2.

3.

4.

5.

Lesson 5   Division (facts through 45 ÷ 5)

$$\begin{array}{r} 8 \\ \times 1 \\ \hline 8 \end{array} \qquad \begin{array}{r} 8 \\ 1\overline{)\,8} \end{array}$$

$$\begin{array}{r} 15 \\ \times 1 \\ \hline 15 \end{array} \qquad \begin{array}{r} 15 \\ 1\overline{)\,15} \end{array}$$

If $1 \times 8 = 8$, then $8 \div 1 = 8$. | If $1 \times 15 = 15$, then _____ $\div 1 =$ _____.

Divide.

	a		*b*	
1.	$\begin{array}{r} 5 \\ \times 1 \\ \hline 5 \end{array}$ $1\overline{)\,5}$		$\begin{array}{r} 14 \\ \times 1 \\ \hline 14 \end{array}$ $1\overline{)\,1\,4}$	
2.	$\begin{array}{r} 4 \\ \times 1 \\ \hline 4 \end{array}$ $1\overline{)\,4}$		$\begin{array}{r} 9 \\ \times 1 \\ \hline 9 \end{array}$ $1\overline{)\,9}$	

	a	*b*	*c*	*d*	*e*
3.	$1\overline{)\,4}$	$1\overline{)\,3}$	$1\overline{)\,1\,2}$	$1\overline{)\,2}$	$1\overline{)\,1\,6}$
4.	$2\overline{)\,8}$	$3\overline{)\,1\,8}$	$2\overline{)\,1\,8}$	$2\overline{)\,6}$	$3\overline{)\,6}$
5.	$4\overline{)\,1\,6}$	$2\overline{)\,1\,4}$	$1\overline{)\,9}$	$5\overline{)\,5}$	$5\overline{)\,4\,5}$
6.	$2\overline{)\,1\,6}$	$4\overline{)\,1\,2}$	$2\overline{)\,1\,0}$	$4\overline{)\,2\,8}$	$1\overline{)\,1\,8}$
7.	$4\overline{)\,4}$	$4\overline{)\,2\,0}$	$5\overline{)\,1\,0}$	$5\overline{)\,3\,0}$	$4\overline{)\,3\,2}$

CHAPTER 11

Lesson 5 Problem Solving

Solve each problem.

1. Dana bought 16 rolls. The rolls came in two packs. The same number of rolls were in each pack. How many rolls were in each pack?

   Dana bought _____ rolls.

   These rolls filled _____ packs.

   There were _____ rolls in each pack.

2. There are nine families in an apartment building. There are three families on each floor. How many floors are in the building?

   There are _____ families in the building.

   There are _____ families on each floor.

   There are _____ floors in the building.

3. Arlene put 36 oranges in bags. She put 4 oranges in each bag. How many bags did she fill?

   Arlene put _____ oranges in bags.

   She put _____ oranges in each bag.

   Arlene filled _____ bags with oranges.

4. Marcos read 35 pages of his science book in five days. He read the same number of pages each day. How many pages did he read each day?

   Marcos read _____ pages each day.

5. Mrs. Allan worked 25 hours in five days. She worked the same number of hours each day. How many hours did she work each day?

   Mrs. Allan worked _____ hours each day.

1.

2.

3.

4.

5.

CHAPTER 11 PRACTICE TEST
Division (basic facts through 45 ÷ 5)

Divide.

	a	*b*	*c*	*d*	*e*
1.	2)̅1̅0̅	1)̅4̅	3)̅3̅	3)̅9̅	2)̅1̅6̅
2.	1)̅1̅2̅	2)̅1̅2̅	3)̅1̅2̅	2)̅1̅4̅	3)̅1̅5̅
3.	3)̅6̅	1)̅8̅	5)̅2̅0̅	1)̅9̅	3)̅2̅4̅
4.	5)̅4̅0̅	5)̅5̅	1)̅1̅0̅	4)̅3̅6̅	4)̅2̅4̅

Solve each problem.

5. The 45 students in a class separated into five groups. Each group has the same number of students. How many are in each group?

There are _____ students in all.

The students are separated into _____ groups.

There are _____ students in each group.

5.

6. Sydney has 28 balloons for a party. She will give each person 4 balloons. How many people will receive balloons?

_____ people will receive balloons.

6.

7. Mr. Graham has six birds. How many cages does he need in order to put two birds in each cage?

Mr. Graham needs _____ cages.

7.

CHAPTER 12 PRETEST
Division (basic facts through 81 ÷ 9)

Divide.

	a	b	c	d	e
1.	6)24	6)12	6)18	6)0	6)6
2.	6)42	6)54	6)30	6)36	6)48
3.	7)0	7)28	7)14	7)21	7)7
4.	7)56	7)42	7)63	7)35	7)49
5.	8)8	8)40	8)0	8)32	8)16
6.	8)24	8)48	8)64	8)72	8)56
7.	9)36	9)27	9)45	9)18	9)0
8.	9)72	9)63	9)54	9)9	9)81
9.	5)5	4)28	1)1	5)30	4)12

Lesson 1 Division (facts through 54 ÷ 6)

$$\begin{array}{r} 3 \\ \times 6 \\ \hline 18 \end{array} \longrightarrow 6\overline{)18}^{\,3}$$

$$\begin{array}{r} 4 \\ \times 6 \\ \hline 24 \end{array} \longrightarrow 6\overline{)24}^{\,4}$$

If 6 × 3 = 18, then 18 ÷ 6 = 3. | If 6 × 4 = 24, then _____ ÷ 6 = _____.

Divide.

	a		*b*	
1.	$\begin{array}{r} 2 \\ \times 6 \\ \hline 12 \end{array}$	$6\overline{)12}$	$\begin{array}{r} 1 \\ \times 6 \\ \hline 6 \end{array}$	$6\overline{)6}$
2.	$\begin{array}{r} 5 \\ \times 6 \\ \hline 30 \end{array}$	$6\overline{)30}$	$\begin{array}{r} 7 \\ \times 6 \\ \hline 42 \end{array}$	$6\overline{)42}$
3.	$\begin{array}{r} 8 \\ \times 6 \\ \hline 48 \end{array}$	$6\overline{)48}$	$\begin{array}{r} 9 \\ \times 6 \\ \hline 54 \end{array}$	$6\overline{)54}$

	a	*b*	*c*	*d*
4.	$6\overline{)6}$	$6\overline{)12}$	$6\overline{)36}$	$6\overline{)18}$
5.	$1\overline{)6}$	$6\overline{)0}$	$6\overline{)24}$	$6\overline{)42}$
6.	$6\overline{)30}$	$6\overline{)54}$	$6\overline{)48}$	$5\overline{)45}$
7.	$4\overline{)32}$	$5\overline{)20}$	$4\overline{)20}$	$5\overline{)30}$

Lesson 1 Problem Solving

Solve each problem.

1. There are six rows of mailboxes. Each row has the same number of mailboxes. There are 30 mailboxes in all. How many are in each row?

There are _____ mailboxes in all.

The mailboxes are separated into _____ rows.

There are _____ mailboxes in each row.

2. The movie was shown 12 times in six days. It was shown the same number of times each day. How many times was it shown each day?

The movie was shown _____ times in all.

The movie was shown for _____ days.

The movie was shown _____ times each day.

3. Jill bought 18 buttons. The buttons were on cards of 6 buttons each. How many cards were there?

Jill bought _____ buttons.

There were _____ buttons on a card.

There were _____ cards.

4. Spencer got six hits in six games. He got the same number of hits in each game. How many hits did he get in each game?

Spencer got _____ hit in each game.

5. One side of a building has 24 windows. Each floor has 6 windows on that side. How many floors does the building have?

The building has _____ floors.

1.
2.
3.
4.
5.

Lesson 2   Division (facts through 64 ÷ 8)

$$3 \cdots\cdots\rightarrow 3$$
$$\times 7 \cdots\cdots\rightarrow 7\overline{)21}$$
$$\overline{21} \cdots\cdots\cdots\uparrow$$

$$5 \cdots\cdots\rightarrow 5$$
$$\times 8 \cdots\cdots\rightarrow 8\overline{)40}$$
$$\overline{40} \cdots\cdots\cdots\uparrow$$

If $7 \times 3 = 21$, then $21 \div 7 = 3$. | If $8 \times 5 = 40$, then _____ ÷ 8 = _____.

Divide.

	a			*b*	
1.	$\times 7$ over 2, $\overline{14}$	$7\overline{)14}$		$\times 8$ over 3, $\overline{24}$	$8\overline{)24}$
2.	$\times 7$ over 5, $\overline{35}$	$7\overline{)35}$		$\times 8$ over 4, $\overline{32}$	$8\overline{)32}$
3.	$\times 7$ over 7, $\overline{49}$	$7\overline{)49}$		$\times 8$ over 8, $\overline{64}$	$8\overline{)64}$

	a	*b*	*c*	*d*
4.	$7\overline{)7}$	$8\overline{)0}$	$8\overline{)16}$	$7\overline{)28}$
5.	$8\overline{)48}$	$7\overline{)42}$	$8\overline{)8}$	$7\overline{)56}$
6.	$7\overline{)0}$	$8\overline{)56}$	$1\overline{)7}$	$7\overline{)63}$
7.	$1\overline{)8}$	$8\overline{)40}$	$8\overline{)72}$	$7\overline{)21}$

Lesson 2 Problem Solving

Solve each problem.

1. A classroom has 28 chairs in seven rows. Each row has the same number of chairs. How many chairs are in each row?

   There are _____ chairs in the classroom.

   The chairs are separated into _____ rows.

   There are _____ chairs in each row.

   1.

2. There are 48 chairs around the tables in the library. There are 8 chairs for each table. How many tables are in the library?

   There are _____ chairs in the library.

   There are _____ chairs around each table.

   There are _____ tables in the library.

   2.

3. Zane worked the same number of hours each day. He worked 21 hours in seven days. How many hours did he work each day?

   Zane worked _____ hours each day.

   3.

4. There are 16 cars in the parking lot. There are 8 cars in each row. How many rows of cars are there?

   There are _____ rows of cars.

   4.

5. Mr. Miller sold seven cars in seven days. He sold the same number of cars each day. How many did he sell each day?

   Mr. Miller sold _____ car each day.

   5.

Lesson 3 Division (facts through 81 ÷ 9)

$$\begin{array}{r} 2 \\ \times 9 \\ \hline 18 \end{array} \longrightarrow \begin{array}{r} 2 \\ 9)\overline{18} \end{array}$$

$$\begin{array}{r} 7 \\ \times 9 \\ \hline 63 \end{array} \longrightarrow \begin{array}{r} 7 \\ 9)\overline{63} \end{array}$$

If $9 \times 2 = 18$, then $18 \div 9 = 2$. | If $9 \times 7 = 63$, then _____ $\div 9 =$ _____.

Divide.

	a			*b*	

1. $\begin{array}{r} 5 \\ \times 9 \\ \hline 45 \end{array}$ $9)\overline{45}$ $\begin{array}{r} 3 \\ \times 9 \\ \hline 27 \end{array}$ $9)\overline{27}$

2. $\begin{array}{r} 8 \\ \times 9 \\ \hline 72 \end{array}$ $9)\overline{72}$ $\begin{array}{r} 4 \\ \times 9 \\ \hline 36 \end{array}$ $9)\overline{36}$

3. $\begin{array}{r} 6 \\ \times 9 \\ \hline 54 \end{array}$ $9)\overline{54}$ $\begin{array}{r} 9 \\ \times 9 \\ \hline 81 \end{array}$ $9)\overline{81}$

a	*b*	*c*	*d*

4. $9)\overline{9}$ $1)\overline{9}$ $9)\overline{18}$ $9)\overline{36}$

5. $9)\overline{0}$ $9)\overline{72}$ $9)\overline{54}$ $9)\overline{81}$

6. $8)\overline{72}$ $9)\overline{63}$ $8)\overline{48}$ $9)\overline{45}$

7. $9)\overline{27}$ $8)\overline{56}$ $7)\overline{63}$ $7)\overline{49}$

CHAPTER 12

Lesson 3   Problem Solving

Solve each problem.

1. A farmer planted 54 cherry trees in nine rows. Each row had the same number of trees. How many trees were in each row?

   A farmer planted _____ trees.

   There were _____ rows of trees.

   There were _____ trees in each row.

2. Curt put 27 tennis balls in nine cans. He put the same number of balls in each can. How many balls did Curt put in each can?

   Curt put _____ tennis balls in cans.

   There were _____ cans.

   He put _____ balls in each can.

3. There are nine packs of batteries on a shelf. Each pack has the same number of batteries. There are 36 batteries in all. How many batteries are in each pack?

   There are _____ batteries in each pack.

4. There are 18 cornstalks in a garden. There are 9 stalks in each row. How many rows of cornstalks are there?

   There are _____ rows of cornstalks.

5. Kay had 45 pennies. She put the pennies into stacks of 9 pennies each. How many stacks of pennies did she make?

   She made _____ stacks of pennies.

1.

2.

3.

4.

5.

Lesson 4 Division Review

Divide.

	a	b	c	d
1.	$2\overline{)10}$	$3\overline{)18}$	$4\overline{)4}$	$1\overline{)8}$
2.	$5\overline{)15}$	$8\overline{)16}$	$6\overline{)24}$	$7\overline{)42}$
3.	$2\overline{)18}$	$3\overline{)24}$	$7\overline{)35}$	$9\overline{)0}$
4.	$5\overline{)25}$	$4\overline{)32}$	$9\overline{)27}$	$6\overline{)36}$
5.	$7\overline{)14}$	$3\overline{)15}$	$8\overline{)8}$	$2\overline{)16}$
6.	$9\overline{)18}$	$6\overline{)12}$	$3\overline{)12}$	$8\overline{)24}$
7.	$5\overline{)20}$	$4\overline{)12}$	$2\overline{)6}$	$5\overline{)10}$
8.	$7\overline{)56}$	$3\overline{)21}$	$8\overline{)40}$	$6\overline{)30}$
9.	$4\overline{)28}$	$9\overline{)45}$	$7\overline{)49}$	$9\overline{)72}$
10.	$8\overline{)64}$	$9\overline{)54}$	$8\overline{)48}$	$9\overline{)81}$

CHAPTER '12

Lesson 4 Problem Solving

Solve each problem.

1. Olivia has 42 apples. She puts 6 apples in a package. How many packages will she have?

Olivia has _____ apples.

She puts _____ apples in each package.

There will be _____ packages of apples.

2. Olivia has 63 peaches. She puts 7 peaches in a package. How many packages will she have?

Olivia has _____ peaches.

Each package will have _____ peaches.

There will be _____ packages of peaches.

3. There are eight packages of pears. Each package has the same number of pears. There are 64 pears in all. How many pears are in each package?

There are _____ pears in all.

There are _____ packages of pears.

There are _____ pears in each package.

1.

2.

3.

CHAPTER 12 PRACTICE TEST
Division (basic facts through 81 ÷ 9)

Divide.

	a	b	c	d	e
1.	$6\overline{)12}$	$7\overline{)7}$	$8\overline{)24}$	$6\overline{)36}$	$9\overline{)0}$
2.	$7\overline{)14}$	$9\overline{)45}$	$6\overline{)42}$	$8\overline{)32}$	$1\overline{)9}$
3.	$6\overline{)48}$	$7\overline{)21}$	$8\overline{)40}$	$9\overline{)18}$	$8\overline{)72}$
4.	$8\overline{)64}$	$9\overline{)81}$	$7\overline{)56}$	$6\overline{)54}$	$6\overline{)18}$
5.	$6\overline{)30}$	$7\overline{)28}$	$9\overline{)72}$	$7\overline{)63}$	$8\overline{)48}$

Solve each problem.

6. A classroom has 24 desks. They are in six rows. There is the same number of desks in each row. How many desks are in each row?

There are _____ desks in all.

There are _____ rows with the same number of desks in each row.

There are _____ desks in each row.

6.

7. Lyle put 24 biscuits on a tray. He put 8 biscuits in each row. How many rows were there?

There were _____ rows.

7.

CHAPTER 12

CHAPTER 13 PRETEST
Metric Measurement

Find the length of each object to the nearest centimeter.

1. _____ centimeters

2. _____ centimeters

3. _____ centimeters

4. _____ centimeters

5. _____ centimeters

How many liters would each container hold?
Ring the best answer.

	a		b		c
6.	1 liter		1 liter		4 liters
	10 liters		5 liters		16 liters
	50 liters		50 liters		80 liter

Solve.

7. A car can go 6 kilometers on a liter of gasoline.
The car has a tank that holds 55 liters. How far
can the car go on a full tank of gasoline?

7.

The car can go _____ kilometers.

Lesson 1 Centimeter

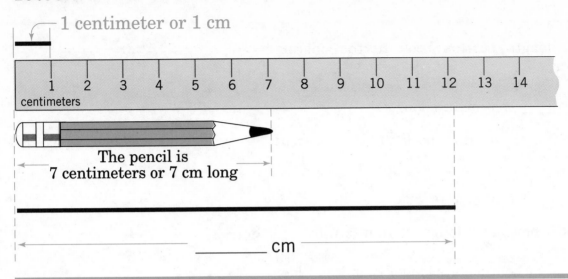

1 centimeter or 1 cm

The pencil is
7 centimeters or 7 cm long

_____ cm

Estimate how long each object is in centimeters.
Then find the length of each object to the nearest centimeter.

1. Estimate: _____ cm

Length: _____ cm

2. Estimate: _____ cm

Length: _____ cm

3. Estimate: _____ cm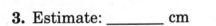

Length: _____ cm

4. Estimate: _____ cm

Length: _____ cm

5. Estimate: _____ cm

Length: _____ cm

6. Estimate: _____ cm

Length: _____ cm

CHAPTER 13

Lesson 1 Problem Solving

Solve each problem.

1. Find the length of this book to the nearest centimeter.

   It is _____ centimeters long.

2. Find the width of this book to the nearest centimeter.

   It is _____ centimeters wide.

3. This book is how much longer than it is wide?

   It is _____ centimeters longer than it is wide.

4. How many centimeters is it across a nickel?

   It is _____ centimeters across.

5. How many centimeters would it be across eight nickels laid in a row?

   It would be _____ centimeters across.

6. Find the length of your shoe to the nearest centimeter.

   It is _____ centimeters long.

Use a tape measure or string to find the following to the nearest centimeter.

7. the distance around your wrist   _____ centimeters

8. the distance around your waist   _____ centimeters

9. the distance around your head   _____ centimeters

10. the distance around your ankle   _____ centimeters

1.	2.
3.	4.
5.	6.

Lesson 2 Measuring (centimeters)

From *A* to *B* is a length of 12 centimeters.

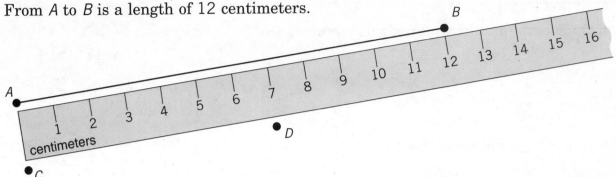

Draw a line from *C* to *D*. It is _____ centimeters long.

---

1. Draw from *E* to *F*.

The length is _____ centimeters.

2. Draw from *G* to *H*.

The length is _____ centimeters.

3. Draw from *J* to *K*.

The length is _____ centimeters.

Complete the table.

	From	*Length*
4.	A to B	_____ cm
5.	B to C	_____ cm
6.	C to D	_____ cm
7.	D to E	_____ cm
8.	E to A	_____ cm
9.	A to D	_____ cm
10.	C to E	_____ cm

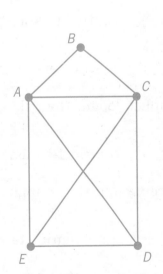

CHAPTER 13

Lesson 2 Problem Solving

Solve each problem.

1. Find the length and the width of this rectangle to the nearest centimeter.

   It is _____ centimeters long.

   It is _____ centimeters wide.

2. The rectangle is how much longer than it is wide?

   It is _____ centimeters longer than it is wide.

3. Find the distance around the rectangle.

   The distance is _____ centimeters.

4. Draw from A to B, from B to C, and from C to A. Then find the length of each side of the triangle you just drew.

   Side AB is _____ centimeters long.

   Side BC is _____ centimeters long.

   Side CA is _____ centimeters long.

5. Side CA is how much longer than side BC?

   Side CA is _____ centimeters longer.

6. Find the distance around the triangle.

   The distance is _____ centimeters.

7. One side of a square is 8 centimeters long. What is the distance around the square? (All four sides of a square are the same length.)

   The distance is _____ centimeters.

A •

• B

C •

Lesson 3 Liter

is about the same as

1 liter is a little more than 1 quart.

Answer *Yes* or *No*.

1. You can put 1 quart of water in a 1-liter bottle. _____

2. You can put 3 liters of water in a 3-quart pail. _____

How many liters would each container hold?
Underline the best answer.

3.

1 liter   8 liters   45 liters

4.

2 liters   9 liters   25 liters

5.

1 liter   10 liters   50 liters

6.

8 liters   28 liters   64 liters

7.

4 liters   16 liters   80 liters

8.

1 liter   4 liters   20 liters

SPECTRUM MATHEMATICS
Red Book

Lesson 3 Problem Solving

Solve each problem.

1. The tank in Mr. Sumner's car can hold 85 liters. It took 37 liters of gasoline to fill the tank. How many liters were in the tank before it was filled?

   _____ liters were in the tank.

2. Mr. Sumner can drive 5 kilometers on each liter of gasoline. How far could he drive on a full tank (85 liters) of gasoline?

   He could drive _____ kilometers on a full tank.

3. Miss Gray uses 17 liters of gasoline to drive to and from work each day. How many liters does she use in six days?

   She uses _____ liters in six days.

4. Evan bought 12 liters of paint. The paint was in three cans of the same size. How many liters of paint were in each can?

   _____ liters of paint were in each can.

5. Chelsea used 56 liters of water to fill eight empty fishbowls. The same amount of water was in each bowl. How many liters were in each fishbowl?

   _____ liters of water were in each fishbowl.

6. A cafeteria serves 95 liters of milk each day. How much milk is served in five days?

   _____ liters of milk is served in five days.

7. Heidi uses 2 liters of gasoline to mow a lawn. She mowed the lawn 16 times this year. How much gasoline did she use to mow the lawn this year?

   Heidi used _____ liters this year.

1.	2.
3.	**4.**
5.	
6.	**7.**

Lesson 4 Metric Weight

A grain of sand weighs
about 1 milligram.

A paper clip weighs
about 1 gram.

A brick weighs
about 1 kilogram.

1 gram = 1,000 milligrams   1,000 grams = 1 kilogram
1 g = 1,000 mg   1,000 g = 1 kg

Use the diagrams above to answer questions **1–5**.

1. What is the weight in grams of ten paper clips?

The weight is _____ grams.

2. What is the weight in grams of 1,000 paper clips?

What is the weight in kilograms?

The weight is _____ grams or _____ kilogram.

3. What is the weight in kilograms of 20 bricks?

The weight is _____ kilograms.

4. What is the weight in milligrams of 100 grains of sand?

The weight is _____ milligrams.

5. Find the weight in milligrams of 2,000 grains of sand. What is the weight in grams?

The weight in milligrams is _____ or _____ grams.

Tell whether you would use milligrams, grams, or kilograms
to measure each of the following.

	a	*b*	*c*
6.	a person _____	a crayon _____	a crumb of bread _____
7.	a granule of sugar _____	a car _____	a cherry _____

CHAPTER
13

Lesson 4 Problem Solving

1. A candy bar has 25 grams of fat. If Randy eats four candy bars, how many grams of fat has he eaten?

   Randy will eat _____ grams of fat.

2. Jose's vitamin tablets weigh 50 milligrams each. If there are five left in the bottle, how many milligrams do they weigh?

   Five tablets weigh _____ milligrams.

3. Bo weighed 50 kilograms at the beginning of the school year. He gained 4 kilograms by the end of the year. What was his weight at the end of the year?

   Bo weighed _____ kilograms at the end of the year.

4. Tamisha had a pack of markers. Each marker weighed 32 grams. There were six markers in the pack. How much did they weigh in all?

   The six markers weighed _____ grams.

5. Kelly's dog weighs 12 kilograms. Julie's dog weighs 10 kilograms. How much do their dogs weigh together?

   Together, their dogs weigh _____ kilograms.

6. Carlos had a bag of cookies in his lunch. Each cookie weighed 20 grams. If there are four cookies in his bag, how much do they weigh in all?

   The cookies weigh _____ grams in all.

7. Kristin bought three computers for her house. They each weigh 35 kilograms. What is the total weight of the three computers?

   _____ kilograms is the total weight.

1.

2.

3.

4.

5.

6.

7.

CHAPTER 13 PRACTICE TEST
Metric Measurement

Find each length to the nearest centimeter.

1. _____ cm

2. _____ cm

Draw from *A* to *B*, from *B* to *C*, and from *C* to *A*.
Then find each length to the nearest centimeter.

B•

3. From *A* to *B* is _____ centimeters.

4. From *B* to *C* is _____ centimeters.

5. From *C* to *A* is _____ centimeters.

A•

•
C

Would you use milligrams, grams, or kilograms to weigh
each of the following? Ring the best answer.

6.   milligrams

grams

kilograms

  milligrams

grams

kilograms

  milligrams

grams

kilograms

Solve each problem.

7. A car can go 8 kilometers on 1 liter of gasoline.
How far could the car go on 40 liters?

The car could go _____ kilometers.

7.

8. Joey had a pack of crayons in his desk. Each
crayon weighed 5 grams. If he had six crayons in
his pack, how much did the crayons weigh in all?

The crayons weighed _____ grams in all.

8.

9. Jenny drinks 2 liters of water each day. How
much water does she drink in seven days?

Jenny drinks _____ liters of water in seven days.

9.

CHAPTER 14 PRETEST
Customary Measurement

Find the length of each object to the nearest inch.

1. _____ inches

2. _____ inch

3. _____ inches

Complete the following.

a

b

4. 1 quart = _____ pints

2 quarts = _____ pints

5. 8 pints = _____ quarts

6 pints = _____ quarts

6. 1 gallon = _____ quarts

3 gallons = _____ quarts

7. 8 quarts = _____ gallons

20 quarts = _____ gallons

8. 1 foot = _____ inches

3 feet = _____ inches

9. 1 yard = _____ feet

1 yard = _____ inches

10. 2 weeks = _____ days

1 hour = _____ minutes

11. 4 weeks = _____ days

6 hours = _____ minutes

12. 1 day = _____ hours

2 days = _____ hours

Solve.

13. Annette bought a board that is 6 feet long. What is the length of the board in inches?

13.

The board is _____ inches long.

Lesson 1 Measuring (inch)

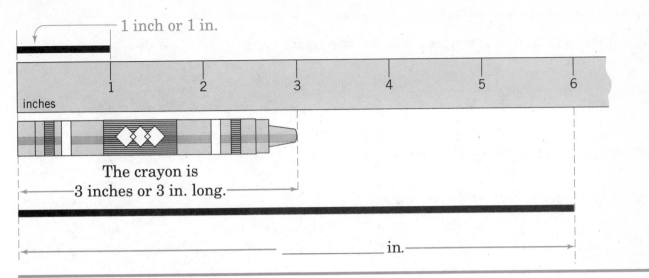

1 inch or 1 in.

inches

The crayon is
3 inches or 3 in. long.

_____ in.

Find the length of each object to the nearest inch.

1. _____ in.

2. _____ in.

3. _____ in.

4. _____ in.

5. _____ in.

Complete the table.

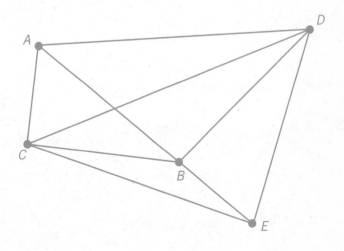

	From	Length
6.	A to B	_____ in.
7.	A to C	_____ in.
8.	B to D	_____ in.
9.	B to E	_____ in.
10.	A to D	_____ in.

Lesson 1 Problem Solving

Solve each problem.

1. Find the length and the width of this book to the nearest inch.

It is _____ inches long.

It is _____ inches wide.

2. Find the length of the blue rectangle.

It is _____ inches long.

3. Find the width of the blue rectangle.

It is _____ inch wide.

4. The rectangle is how much longer than it is wide?

It is _____ inches longer than it is wide.

5. Find the distance around the blue rectangle.

The distance is _____ inches.

6. Draw a line from *R* to *S*, from *S* to *T*, and from *T* to *R*. Then find the length of each side of the triangle.

Side *RS* is _____ inches long.

Side *ST* is _____ inch long.

Side *TR* is _____ inches long.

7. Find the distance around the triangle you drew.

The distance is _____ inches.

Lesson 2 Units of Length

1 foot (ft) = 12 inches (in.)   3 feet (ft) = 1 yard (yd)

3 ft = _____?_____ in.

Since 1 ft = 12 in., then

$$\begin{array}{cc} \downarrow & \downarrow \\ 1 & 12 \\ \times 3 & \times 3 \\ \hline 3 & 36 \\ \downarrow & \downarrow \end{array}$$

3 ft = _36_ in.

12 ft = _____?_____ yd

Since 3 ft = 1 yd, then

$$3\overline{)1\,2}^{\,4}$$

12 ft = _4_ yd

Complete the following.

            a   *b*

1. 6 ft = _____ in.   8 ft = _____ in.

2. 3 yd = _____ ft   8 yd = _____ ft

3. 1 yd = _____ in.   2 yd = _____ in.

4. 21 ft = _____ yd   12 ft = _____ yd

5. 5 yd = _____ ft   14 yd = _____ ft

6. 3 ft = _____ in.   3 yd = _____ in.

7. 7 yd = _____ ft   9 ft = _____ in.

8. 18 ft = _____ yd   11 yd = _____ ft

9. 9 yd = _____ ft   5 ft = _____ in.

10. 7 ft = _____ in.   27 ft = _____ yd

11. 6 yd = _____ ft   15 ft = _____ yd

12. 9 ft = _____ yd   10 yd = _____ ft

Lesson 2   Problem Solving

Solve each problem.

1. Teresa bought 2 yards of ribbon for a dress. How many feet of ribbon did she buy?

   Teresa bought _____ feet of ribbon.

2. Myron bought a belt that was 2 feet long. How long was the belt in inches?

   The belt was _____ inches long.

3. Mark has a rope that is 3 yards long. How long is the rope in feet?

   It is _____ feet long.

4. In problem **3**, how long is the rope in inches?

   It is _____ inches long.

5. Preston has a piece of wire 5 feet long. How long is the wire in inches?

   It is _____ inches long.

6. The distance between two walls is 18 feet. What is this distance in yards?

   It is _____ yards.

7. Pam's driveway is 15 feet wide. How wide is the driveway in yards?

   It is _____ yards wide.

8. A fence post is 4 feet high. How high is the fence post in inches?

   It is _____ inches high.

1.

2.

3.

4.

5.

6.

7.

8.

Lesson 3 Units of Capacity

1 quart (qt) = 2 pints (pt)   2 pints (pt) = 1 quart (qt)

5 qt = __?__ pt

Since 1 qt = 2 pt, then

$$\downarrow \qquad \downarrow$$
$$1 \qquad 2$$
$$\times 5 \qquad \times 5$$
$$\overline{5} \qquad \overline{10}$$
$$\downarrow \qquad \downarrow$$

5 qt = __10__ pt

10 pt = __?__ qt

Since 2 pt = 1 qt, then

10 pt = ____ qt

1 gallon (gal) = 4 qt or 4 qt = 1 gal

12 qt = __?__ gal

Since 4 qt = 1 gal, then

12 qt = ____ gal

Complete the following.

	a	*b*
1.	7 qt = _____ pt	3 qt = _____ pt
2.	8 pt = _____ qt	18 pt = _____ qt
3.	5 gal = _____ qt	2 gal = _____ qt
4.	24 qt = _____ gal	36 qt = _____ gal
5.	4 pt = _____ qt	7 gal = _____ qt
6.	8 qt = _____ pt	20 qt = _____ gal
7.	8 gal = _____ qt	12 pt = _____ qt
8.	28 qt = _____ gal	9 qt = _____ pt
9.	14 pt = _____ qt	9 gal = _____ qt

CHAPTER 14

Lesson 3 Problem Solving

Solve each problem.

1. Mrs. Collins bought 12 quarts of milk last week. How many pints of milk was this?

   It was _____ pints.

2. In problem **1**, how many gallons of milk did Mrs. Collins buy?

   She bought _____ gallons.

3. Mr. Murphy used 24 quarts of paint to paint his house. He bought paint in gallon cans. How many gallons of paint did he use?

   He used _____ gallons of paint.

4. Mr. Johnson sold 18 pints of milk yesterday. How many quarts of milk was this?

   It was _____ quarts of milk.

5. Dominic made 8 quarts of lemonade for a party. How many gallons of lemonade did he make?

   He made _____ gallons of lemonade.

6. Patrick drank 10 pints of milk one week. How many quarts of milk did he drink?

   He drank _____ quarts of milk.

7. Ms. Carlow used 4 gallons of paint. How many quarts of paint did she use?

   She used _____ quarts of paint.

8. How many pint glasses could be filled from 8 quarts of juice?

   _____ pint glasses could be filled.

1.
2.
3.
4.
5.
6.
7.
8.

Lesson 4 Units of Weight

Pounds and ounces measure weight.

1 pound (lb) = 16 ounces (oz)

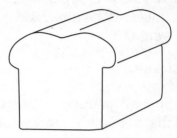

A crayon weighs about an ounce.   A loaf of bread weighs about a pound.

Use the diagrams above to answer questions **1–6.**

1. Which is less, a pound or an ounce? _____

2. Which is more, 1 pound or 10 ounces? _____

3. Which weighs more, 16 ounces of lunchmeat or 1 pound

of lunchmeat? _____

4. Which is more, 20 ounces of cheese or 1 pound

of cheese? _____

5. Would a football be more likely to weigh 2 ounces or 2 pounds? _____

6. Would a bear be more likely to weigh 90 ounces or 90 pounds? _____

Tell whether you would use ounces or pounds to measure each of the following.

	a	*b*	*c*
7.	a paperclip _____	a bicycle _____	a piece of paper _____
8.	a dollar bill _____	a math book _____	a dog _____

CHAPTER 14

Lesson 4 Problem Solving

Solve each problem.

1. A piece of notebook paper from Timmy's folder weighs 2 ounces. If he has 70 pages how much do the pages weigh?

   Seventy pages weigh _____ ounces.

2. A dog weighs 67 pounds with his collar on. The collar weighs 5 pounds How much does the dog weigh without its collar?

   Without its collar, the dog weighs _____ pounds.

3. There are ten croquet balls in a bag. Each ball weighs 2 pounds. How much do all ten balls weigh?

   Ten balls weigh _____ pounds.

4. Alicia has a 20-ounce soda. She drinks 7 ounces of the soda. How much soda is left?

   There are _____ ounces of soda left.

5. Each bottle is filled with 2 ounces of hand lotion. If Mandy has 12 bottles, how many ounces of hand lotion does she have?

   Mandy has _____ ounces of hand lotion.

6. Tommy weighed 85 pounds. After being ill for a week, he lost 8 pounds. How much does Tommy weigh now?

   Tommy weighs _____ pounds now.

7. A large bag of corn weighs 4 pounds. What is the weight in ounces?

   It is _____ ounces.

8. Jeffrey's mom bought 2 pounds of lunchmeat. How many ounces did she buy?

   Jeffrey's mom bought _____ ounces of lunchmeat.

1.

2.

3.

4.

5.

6.

7.

8.

Lesson 5   Units of Time

3 weeks = ____?____ days

1 week = 7 days

↓   ↓

1   7

×3   ×3

_____

3   21

↓   ↓

3 weeks = __21__ days

4 hours = ____?____ min

1 hour = 60 min

4 hours = _____ min

2 days = ____?____ hours

1 day = 24 hours

2 days = _____ hours

Complete the following.

	a	b

1. 2 weeks = _____ days   8 weeks = _____ days

2. 5 hours = _____ min   7 hours = _____ min

3. 6 days = _____ hours   4 days = _____ hours

4. 6 hours = _____ min   9 weeks = _____ days

5. 6 weeks = _____ days   7 days = _____ hours

6. 9 days = _____ hours   3 hours = _____ min

7. 9 hours = _____ min   5 weeks = _____ days

8. 8 days = _____ hours   7 weeks = _____ days

SPECTRUM MATHEMATICS
Red Book

CHAPTER 14

Lesson 5
Units of Time

179

Lesson 5 Problem Solving

Solve each problem.

1. Brad was at camp for five weeks. How many days was he at camp?

1.

There are _____ days in one week.

He was at camp _____ weeks.

He was at camp _____ days.

2. Tanya attends school six hours every school day. How many minutes does she attend every school day?

2.

There are _____ minutes in one hour.

She attends school _____ hours.

She attends school _____ minutes.

3. Holly was in the hospital for four days. How many hours was she in the hospital?

3.

There are _____ hours in one day.

Holly was in the hospital _____ days.

She was in the hospital _____ hours.

4. The Cooke family has lived in their new apartment for six weeks. How many days have they lived in their new apartment?

4.

They have lived there _____ days.

5. Mackenzie was away from home for one week. How many hours was she away from home?

5.

Mackenzie was away from home _____ hours.

Lesson 6 Temperature

A thermometer measures the temperature in degrees Fahrenheit.

The temperature reading on this thermometer is 32 degrees

Fahrenheit. This can be written as 32°F.

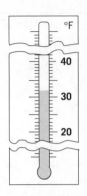

What is the temperature reading on each thermometer?

| | *a* | *b* | *c* |

1.

   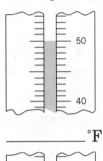

_____ °F   _____ °F   _____ °F

2.

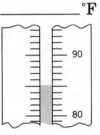

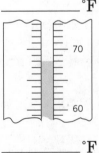

_____ °F   _____ °F   _____ °F

3.

_____ °F   _____ °F   _____ °F

4.

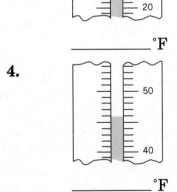

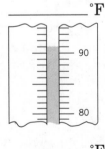

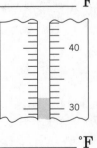

_____ °F   _____ °F   _____ °F

CHAPTER 14

Lesson 6 Problem Solving

Solve each problem.

1. Water freezes at 32°F and boils at 212°F. What is the difference between these two temperatures?

   The difference is _____ degrees.

   1.

2. When Lin went to school in the morning, the temperature was 55°F. By the end of the school day the temperature had risen 20 degrees. What was the temperature at the end of the school day?

   It was _____ °F at the end of the school day.

   2.

3. While Kwasi was ill, his temperature was 102°F. By the next morning his temperature was almost normal, 99°F. How much did his temperature go down?

   His temperature went down _____ degrees.

   3.

4. Rita is going swimming on a hot summer day. The temperature outside is 91°F. The water temperature is 78°F. What is the difference between the air temperature and the water temperature?

   The difference is _____ degrees.

   4.

5. The temperature outside was 87°F. A cold front blew through the area and the temperature dropped 32 degrees. What is the temperature now?

   The temperature is _____ °F.

   5.

6. Tat's refrigerator was set at 45°F. The electricity went off and the temperature rose 14 degrees. What is the temperature in the refrigerator now?

   The temperature is _____ °F.

   6.

7. Inside the air-conditioned house the temperature is 74°F. The temperature outside is 18 degrees warmer. What is the temperature outside?

   The temperature outside is _____ °F.

   7.

Lesson 7 Problem Solving

Solve each problem.

1. A piece of wire is 2 feet long. How long is the wire in inches?

   The wire is _____ inches long.

2. If you use 14 inches of the wire in problem **1**, how many inches are left?

   There will be _____ inches left.

3. On a football field there are 100 yards between goal lines. How many feet is that?

   There are _____ feet between goal lines.

4. A container holds 8 quarts of liquid. How many pints does that container hold?

   That container holds _____ pints.

5. How many gallons of liquid does the container in problem **4** hold?

   That container holds _____ gallons.

6. A telethon lasted two days. How many hours did the telethon last?

   The telethon lasted _____ hours.

7. A television mini-series lasted six hours. How many minutes did the mini-series last?

   The mini-series lasted _____ minutes.

8. The Mohrs spent three weeks on their vacation trip. How many days was that?

   The vacation trip took _____ days.

1.	2.
3.	4.
5.	6.
7.	8.

CHAPTER 14

Lesson 8 Measurement Review

Find each length to the nearest inch.

1. _____ in. _____

2. _____ in. _____

3. _____ in. _____

4. _____ in. _____

Complete the following.

a	*b*

5. 4 ft = _____ in.   4 pt = _____ qt

6. 6 qt = _____ pt   21 ft = _____ yd

7. 8 gal = _____ qt   9 ft = _____ in.

8. 9 yd = _____ ft   36 qt = _____ gal

9. 6 weeks = _____ days   8 hours = _____ min

10. 3 days = _____ hours   8 weeks = _____ days

Solve each problem.

11. Kaylee has a rope 8 feet long. How long is the rope in inches?

    It is _____ inches long.

11.

12. Craig had a gallon of gasoline. He used 1 quart for the lawn mower. How many quarts did he have left?

    He had _____ quarts left.

12.

13. Tonya is 4 feet 11 inches tall. What is her height in inches?

    Her height is _____ inches.

13.

CHAPTER 14 PRACTICE TEST
Customary Measurement

Find the length to the nearest inch.

1. _____ in. _____

2. _____ in. _____

3. _____ in. _____

Complete the following.

             a   *b*

4. 5 ft. = _____ in.   6 pt = _____ qt

5. 10 qt = _____ pt   18 ft = _____ yd

6. 7 gal = _____ qt   3 lb = _____ oz

7. 8 yd = _____ ft   32 qt = _____ gal

8. 5 weeks = _____ days   9 hours = _____ min

9. 4 days = _____ hours   5 lb = _____ oz

What is the temperature reading on each thermometer?

              a   *b*   *c*

10.

_____ °F   _____ °F   _____ °F

Solve each problem.

11. Carmen had a gallon of gasoline. She used 2 quarts for the lawn mower. How many quarts did she have left?

    She had _____ quarts left.

11.

12. Mr. Carpenter's mailbox was 4 feet high. How high is the mailbox in inches?

    It is _____ inches high.

12.

CHAPTER 15 PRETEST
Fractions

What fraction of the figure is shaded?

a	b	c

1.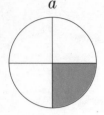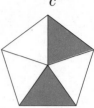

_____   _____   _____

Write an equivalent fraction.

a

2.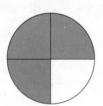

b

$$\frac{3}{4} = \frac{\;}{8}$$

$$\frac{1}{3} = \frac{\;}{\;}$$

Compare the fractions. Use >, <, or =.

a

3.

b

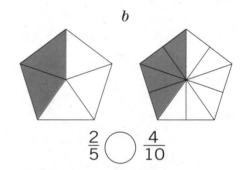

$$\frac{3}{8} \bigcirc \frac{1}{4}$$

$$\frac{2}{5} \bigcirc \frac{4}{10}$$

Order from least to greatest.

a

4.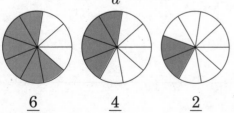

b

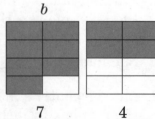

$$\frac{6}{9} \qquad \frac{4}{9} \qquad \frac{2}{9}$$

$$\frac{5}{8} \qquad \frac{7}{8} \qquad \frac{4}{8}$$

_____   _____

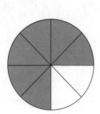

Lesson 1 Fractions of a Whole

A fraction is a number for part of a whole. The top number of a fraction is the numerator. The bottom number is the denominator.

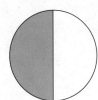 

$\frac{1}{2}$ ← part shaded
$\frac{1}{2}$ ← parts in all

$\frac{2}{3}$ ← parts shaded
$\frac{2}{3}$ ← parts in all

$\frac{1}{2}$ of the circle is shaded blue.

$\frac{2}{3}$ of the rectangle is shaded blue.

What fraction of each figure is shaded?

	a	*b*	*c*

1.

_____ _____ _____

2.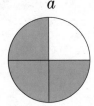

_____ _____ _____

3.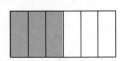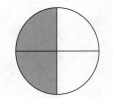

_____ _____ _____

4.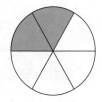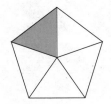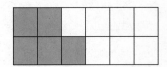

_____ _____ _____

Lesson 2 Fractions of a Set

Write the fraction for the shaded part of the set.

  $\dfrac{1}{3}$ ← number shaded—numerator
← number in all—denominator

$\dfrac{1}{3}$ of the set is shaded blue.

Write the fraction for the shaded part of each set.

| | *a* | *b* | *c* |

1.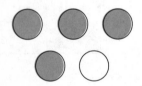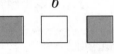

_____   _____   _____

2.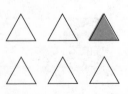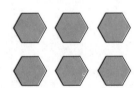

_____   _____   _____

3.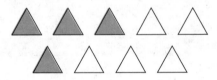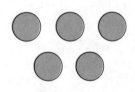

_____   _____   _____

4.

_____   _____   _____

Lesson 3 Equivalent Fractions

Equivalent fractions name the same number.

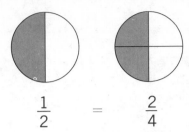

$$\frac{1}{2} \quad = \quad \frac{2}{4}$$

Write an equivalent fraction.

a b

1.

$$\frac{1}{3} = \frac{}{6}$$

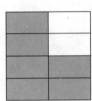

$$\frac{3}{4} = \frac{}{8}$$

2.

$$\frac{2}{5} = \frac{}{10}$$

$$\frac{1}{2} = \frac{}{6}$$

3.

$$\frac{2}{4} = \frac{}{12}$$

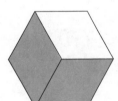

$$\frac{2}{3} = \frac{}{6}$$

4.

$$\frac{7}{8} = \frac{}{16}$$

$$\frac{4}{5} = \frac{}{15}$$

CHAPTER 15

Lesson 3 Problem Solving

Write equivalent fractions.

a   b

1.

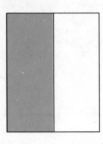 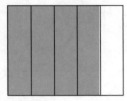

$$\frac{1}{2} = \frac{}{10}$$ $$\frac{2}{3} = \frac{}{12}$$

2.

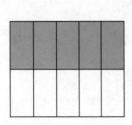 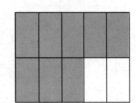    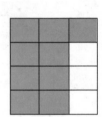

$$\frac{4}{5} = \frac{8}{}$$ $$\frac{}{4} = \frac{9}{12}$$

3.

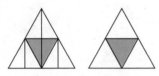   

$$- = -$$ $$- = -$$

4.

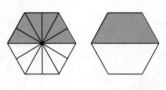

$$- = -$$ $$- = -$$

5.

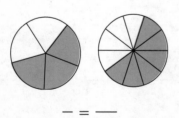

$$- = -$$ $$- = -$$

Lesson 4 Compare Fractions

  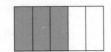 

$$\frac{1}{2} > \frac{1}{3}$$

$\frac{1}{2}$ is greater than $\frac{1}{3}$.

$$\frac{3}{5} < \frac{2}{3}$$

$\frac{3}{5}$ is less than $\frac{2}{3}$.

$$\frac{3}{4} = \frac{6}{8}$$

$\frac{3}{4}$ is equal to $\frac{6}{8}$.

Use >, <, or = to compare the fractions.

	a	*b*	*c*

1.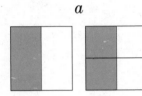

$\frac{1}{2} \bigcirc \frac{2}{4}$ $\frac{1}{5} \bigcirc \frac{1}{3}$ $\frac{2}{8} \bigcirc \frac{2}{5}$

2.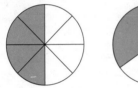

$\frac{4}{8} \bigcirc \frac{1}{3}$ $\frac{3}{5} \bigcirc \frac{9}{15}$ $\frac{2}{3} \bigcirc \frac{5}{6}$

3.

$\frac{7}{8} \bigcirc \frac{3}{4}$ $\frac{4}{6} \bigcirc \frac{6}{9}$ $\frac{9}{10} \bigcirc \frac{3}{4}$

Lesson 5 Order Fractions

Compare the shaded parts of the figures. Then write the fractions in order from least to greatest.

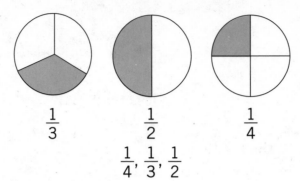

$\frac{1}{3}$ $\frac{1}{2}$ $\frac{1}{4}$

$\frac{1}{4}$, $\frac{1}{3}$, $\frac{1}{2}$

Place the fractions in order from least to greatest.

1.

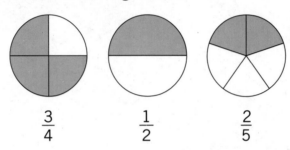

$\frac{3}{4}$ $\frac{1}{2}$ $\frac{2}{5}$

___ , ___ , ___

2.

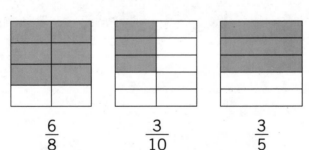

$\frac{6}{8}$ $\frac{3}{10}$ $\frac{3}{5}$

___ , ___ , ___

3.

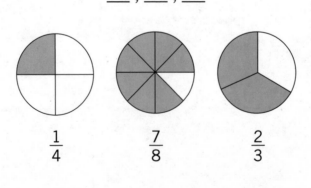

$\frac{1}{4}$ $\frac{7}{8}$ $\frac{2}{3}$

___ , ___ , ___

CHAPTER 15 PRACTICE TEST

What fraction of the figure is shaded?

1.
a
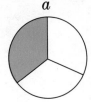

b
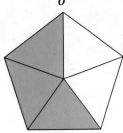

c

_____   _____   _____

Write a number to show equivalent fractions.

2.
a
 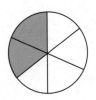

$$\frac{1}{3} = \frac{}{6}$$

b
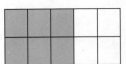

$$\frac{3}{5} = \frac{6}{}$$

Compare the fractions. Use >, <, or =.

3.
a
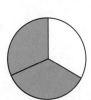

$$\frac{2}{3} \bigcirc \frac{1}{4}$$

b
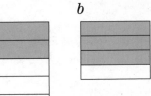

$$\frac{2}{5} \bigcirc \frac{3}{4}$$

Place the fractions in order from least to greatest.

4.
a
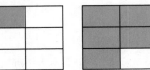

$$\frac{3}{6}, \frac{1}{6}, \frac{5}{6} \quad \text{_____}$$

b
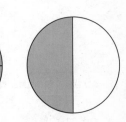

$$\frac{3}{4}, \frac{7}{8}, \frac{1}{2} \quad \text{_____}$$

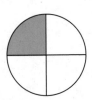
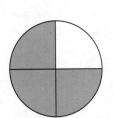

CHAPTER 16 PRETEST
Geometry

Match each figure in column *a* with its name in column *b*.

	a		*b*

1.   cube

2.   triangle

3.   rectangular solid

4.  cylinder

5.   sphere

6.   square

Is the line drawn on each figure a line of symmetry?

       a   *b*   *c*

7. 

_____   _____   _____

8. Find the perimeter and area of the rectangle.

perimeter: _____ inches

area: _____ square inches

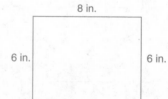

Lesson 1 Plane Figures

The following are plane figures.

circle   triangle   square   rectangle

Each side of a triangle, square, and rectangle is a
line segment. The point where two lines meet is
called a corner.

side →   corner

List the letters of all the figures that apply to each figure name.

1. square _____

2. circle _____

3. triangle _____

4. rectangle _____

  a   b   c

  d  e   f

Complete the table.

	plane figure	number of sides	number of corners
5.	circle	0	
6.	triangle		
7.	square		
8.	rectangle		

9. What do you notice about the number of sides and the number of corners
in each plane figure? _____

_____

10. If a figure has six sides, how many corners does it have? _____

11. If a figure has ten corners, how many sides does it have? _____

CHAPTER 16

Lesson 2 Solid Figures

The following are solid figures.

sphere

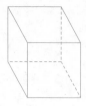

cube

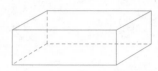

rectangular solid

cone

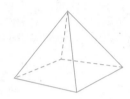

cylinder

pyramid

List the letters of all the figures that apply to each figure name.

1. cone _____

2. cube _____

3. cylinder _____

4. pyramid _____

5. rectangular solid _____

6. sphere _____

a   *b*   *c*

d 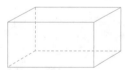   *e*   *f*

g   *h*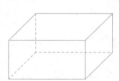

Name the solid figure that each object is shaped like.

<table>
<tr><td>a</td><td>b</td></tr>
<tr><td>7. soup can _____</td><td>basketball _____</td></tr>
<tr><td>8. cereal box _____</td><td>ice-cream cone _____</td></tr>
<tr><td>9. dice _____</td><td>soda can _____</td></tr>
</table>

Lesson 3 Congruence

Two figures are congruent if they are the same shape and the same size.

Which of the following figures is congruent to ?

Figure A   Figure B   Figure C

   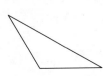   

Figure ___C___ is congruent because it is the same shape and size.

Ring the figure congruent to the first one in each row.

	a	b	c

1.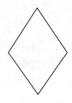

2.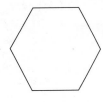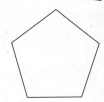

3.

4.    ▭

5.       ◺

6.

CHAPTER 16

Lesson 4 Symmetry

A line of symmetry is a line on which a figure can be folded so that both parts are congruent.

This figure has a line of symmetry.

This figure does not have a line of symmetry.

Is the line drawn on each figure a line of symmetry?

a	*b*	*c*

1.

_____ _____ _____

2.

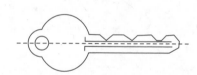

_____ _____ _____

Does each figure have a line of symmetry? If so, draw the line of symmetry.

a	*b*	*c*

3.

_____ _____ _____

4.

_____ _____ _____

Lesson 5 Perimeter

Perimeter is the distance around a figure.
You can find perimeter by adding the measures of all the sides.

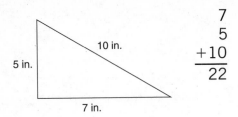

$$\begin{array}{r} 7 \\ 5 \\ +10 \\ \hline 22 \end{array}$$

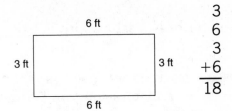

$$\begin{array}{r} 3 \\ 6 \\ 3 \\ +6 \\ \hline 18 \end{array}$$

The perimeter is ___22___ inches.

The perimeter is ___18___ feet.

Find the perimeter of each figure.

a

b

1.

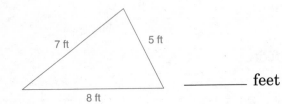

_____ feet

_____ centimeters

2.

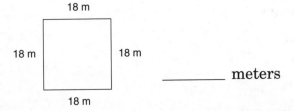

_____ meters

_____ inches

3.

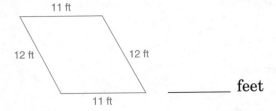

_____ feet

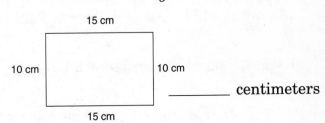

_____ centimeters

4.

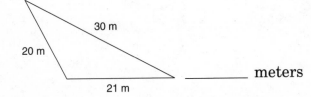

_____ meters

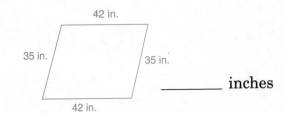

_____ inches

Lesson 5 Problem Solving

1. Kenesha is flying a kite that is shaped like a triangle. The sides of the kite are 4 feet, 3 feet, and 3 feet long. What is the perimeter of her kite?

   The perimeter of Kenesha's kite is _____ feet.

2. The Wessels' swimming pool is shaped like a rectangle. It is 7 meters long and 5 meters wide. What is the perimeter of the Wessels' pool?

   The perimeter of the swimming pool is _____ meters.

3. Paul is planting a rectangular garden in his backyard. The garden will be 13 feet long and 8 feet wide. What will be the perimeter of Paul's garden?

   The perimeter of the garden will be _____ feet.

4. The Turners have a sailboat. The sail on the boat is shaped like a triangle. The sides of the sail measure 22 feet, 12 feet, and 25 feet. What is the perimeter of the sail on the Turners' sailboat?

   The perimeter of the sail is _____ feet.

5. Tristann made a rectangular blanket for her baby cousin. The blanket is 48 inches long and 31 inches wide. What is the perimeter of the blanket?

   The perimeter of the blanket is _____ inches.

1.

2.

3.

4.

5.

Lesson 6 Area of a Rectangle

Area is the number of square units it takes to cover the figure.
You can find the area of a rectangle by multiplying the length times the width.

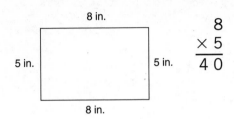

$$\begin{array}{r} 8 \\ \times\ 5 \\ \hline 4\,0 \end{array}$$

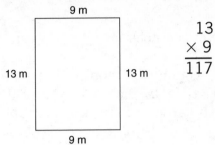

$$\begin{array}{r} 13 \\ \times\ 9 \\ \hline 117 \end{array}$$

The area is ___40___ square inches.

The area is ___117___ square meters.

Find the area of each rectangle.

a

b

1.

_____ square centimeters

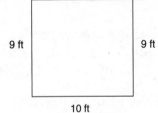

_____ square feet

2.

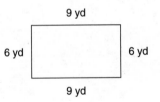

_____ square yards

_____ square inches

3.

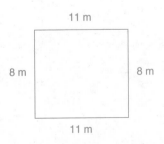

_____ square meters

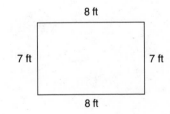

_____ square feet

Lesson 6 Problem Solving

1. Mr. Kwan built a rectangular deck in his backyard. The deck is 7 yards by 9 yards. What is the area of the deck?

The area of the deck is _____ square yards.

1.

2. Patrick's computer monitor is shaped like a rectangle. It is 16 inches long and 9 inches high. What is the area of Patrick's computer monitor?

The area is _____ square inches.

2.

3. The Williams family owns a farm. The farm is shaped like a rectangle. It is 8 kilometers by 4 kilometers. What is the area of the farm?

The area of the farm is _____ square kilometers.

3.

4. Kenya is putting new carpeting in her bedroom. Her bedroom is 13 feet long and 9 feet wide. How many square feet of carpet does Kenya need?

Kenya needs _____ square feet of carpet.

4.

5. Measure the rectangle using a centimeter ruler. Then find the area of the rectangle.

5.

The rectangle is _____ centimeters long.

The rectangle is _____ centimeters wide.

The area of the rectangle is _____ square centimeters.

CHAPTER 16 PRACTICE TEST
Geometry

Name each figure.

a   b   c

1.

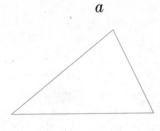   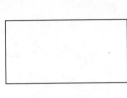   

_____   _____   _____

2.

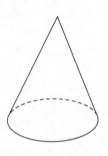   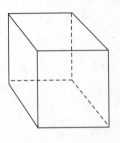

_____   _____   _____

Does each figure have a line of symmetry? If so, draw the line of symmetry.

a   b   c

3.

_____   _____   _____

Find the perimeter of each figure.

a   b

4.

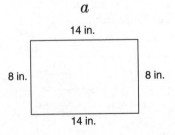   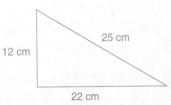

14 in.
8 in.   8 in.
14 in.

12 cm   25 cm   22 cm

_____ inches   _____ centimeters

5. What is the area of the rectangle in problem **4a**? _____ square inches

CHAPTER 17 PRETEST
Graphs and Probability

Use the bar graph to answer each question.

1. How many students chose bananas as their favorite fruit? _____ students

2. How many students chose oranges as their favorite fruit? _____ students

3. What fruit did 12 students choose as their favorite? _____

4. What fruit did 18 students choose as their favorite? _____

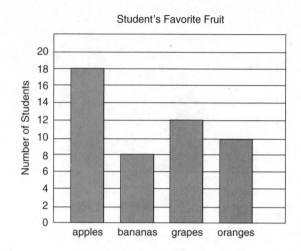

Student's Favorite Fruit

Use the picture graph to answer each question.

5. How many home runs did Kareem hit? _____

6. How many home runs did Carlos hit? _____

7. Which player hit 13 home runs? _____

8. Which two players hit the same number of home runs? _____

9. How many more home runs did Carlos hit than David? _____

Number of Home Runs in the Baseball Season

Justin	⊙ ⊙ ⊙ ⊙
Carlos	⊙ ⊙ ⊙ ⊙ ⊙ ⊙ ⊙ (
Kareem	⊙ ⊙ ⊙ ⊙
David	⊙ ⊙ ⊙ ⊙ ⊙ (

key: ⊙ = 2 home runs

Use the line graph to answer each question.

10. After 40 minutes, how many miles did D.J. run? _____ miles

11. After 80 minutes, how many miles did D.J. run? _____ miles

12. After how many minutes had D.J. run 8 miles? _____ minutes

13. What is the greatest number of miles that D.J. ran in a 20-minute period? _____ miles

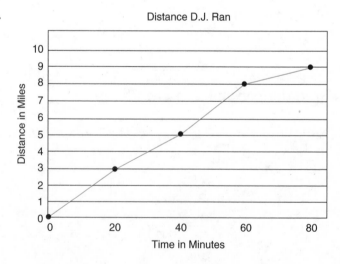

Distance D.J. Ran

Lesson 1 Bar Graphs

A **bar graph** uses rectangular bars to represent data. The *scale* of a bar graph helps you identify the value of each bar.

How many students take the bus to school at Oakdale Elementary School?

Find the bar labeled *Bus.*

Follow the top of the bar to the scale at the left. This value represents the number of students that take the bus to school.

_60_ students take the bus to school.

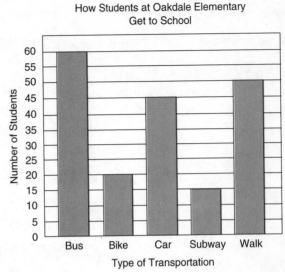

How Students at Oakdale Elementary Get to School

Use the bar graph to answer each question.

1. How many students ride in a car to school?   _____ students

2. How many students take the subway to school?   _____ students

3. How many students walk to school?   _____ students

4. What type of transportation do twenty students take to school?   _____

5. How many more students walk to school than ride a bike to school?   _____ students

6. How many total students take the bus or the subway to school?   _____ students

7. What type of transportation do the fewest students use to get
   to school?   _____

8. What type of transportation do the most students use to get
   to school?   _____

9. What types of transportation do more than 40 students use to get
   to school?   _____

10. If 10 more students were added to the bar labeled *Car,* which type
    of transportation would the most students use to get to school?   _____

CHAPTER 17

Lesson 1 Bar Graphs

Use the bar graph to answer each question.

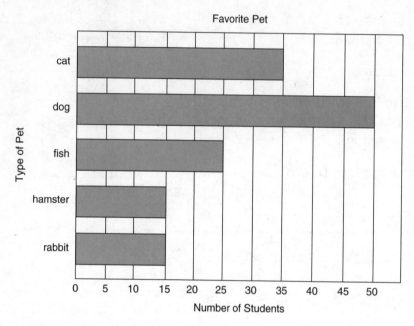

Favorite Pet

1. What type of pet(s) did most students choose as their favorite?

_____

2. What type of pet(s) did the fewest students choose as their favorite?

_____

3. How many students chose a hamster as their favorite pet? _____ students

4. How many students chose a cat as their favorite pet? _____ students

5. How many students chose a dog as their favorite pet? _____ students

6. How many students chose a rabbit as their favorite pet? _____ students

7. What type of pet did 25 students choose as their favorite pet? _____

8. Which two types of pets did the same number of students choose as their favorite?

_____

9. How many more students chose a fish as their favorite pet than a hamster?

_____ students

10. How many total students chose a dog or a cat as their favorite pet?

_____ students

Lesson 2 Picture Graphs

A **picture graph** uses symbols to represent data.
The *key* tells you the value of each symbol on the picture graph.

How many students chose vanilla as their favorite ice-cream flavor?

Students' Favorite Ice-Cream Flavor

chocolate	🍦🍦🍦🍦🍦
chocolate chip	🍦🍦🍦🍦🍦🍦🍦🍦🍦🍦
cookies & cream	🍦🍦🍦🍦🍦🍦🍦
strawberry	🍦🍦🍦
vanilla	🍦🍦🍦🍦🍦🍦

key: 🍦 = 2 students

Each ice-cream cone represents two students.
Count by 2s when counting the ice-cream cones in the row labeled "vanilla."

__12__ students chose vanilla ice cream.

Use the picture graph to answer each question.

1. What ice-cream flavor did most students choose as their favorite? _____

2. What ice-cream flavor did the fewest students choose as their favorite? _____

3. How many students chose chocolate chip as their favorite ice-cream flavor? _____ students

4. How many students chose strawberry as their favorite ice-cream flavor? _____ students

5. What flavor did 16 students choose as their favorite ice-cream flavor? _____

6. What flavor did 11 students choose as their favorite ice-cream flavor? _____

Lesson 2 Picture Graphs

Use the picture graph
to answer each question.

People Attending School Play

Thursday Evening	☺☺☺☺☺
Friday Evening	☺☺☺☺☺☺☺☺
Saturday Afternoon	☺☺☺☺☺☺☺☺
Saturday Evening	☺☺☺☺☺☺☺☺☺☺☺☺☺
Sunday Afternoon	☺☺☺☺☺☺☺

key: ☺ = 10 people

1. Which show did most people attend? _____

2. Which show did the fewest people attend? _____

3. How many people attended the Friday evening show? _____ people

4. How many people attended the Thursday evening show? _____ people

5. How many people attended the Saturday afternoon show? _____ people

6. Which show did 70 people attend? _____

7. Which show did 125 people attend? _____

8. Which two shows had the same number of people in attendance? _____ _____

9. How many more people attended the show on Saturday afternoon than Sunday afternoon? _____ people

10. How many more people attended the show on Saturday evening than Friday evening? _____ people

11. If there was a show on Sunday evening and 90 people attended that show, how many symbols would there be for Sunday evening? _____ symbols

12. If there was a show on Monday evening and 65 people attended that show, how many symbols would there be for Monday evening? _____ symbols

Lesson 3 Line Graphs

A **line graph** uses a line to show how data changes over a period of time.
Each *point* on the graph represents a data value at a given time.

How many tomatoes did Beth pick
by the end of June?

Locate the point that represents
the end of June. Follow this point
to the scale at the left. This value
represents the number of tomatoes
picked by the end of June.

Beth picked ___15___ tomatoes by the
end of June.

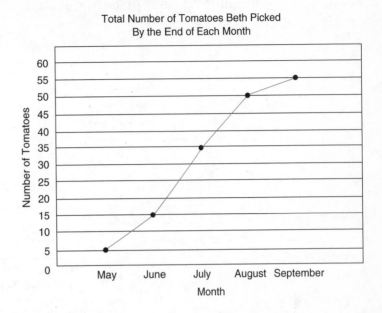

Total Number of Tomatoes Beth Picked
By the End of Each Month

Use the line graph to answer each question.

1. How many tomatoes did Beth pick by the end of May?   _____ tomatoes

2. How many tomatoes did Beth pick by the end of September?   _____ tomatoes

3. By the end of what month did Beth pick 50 tomatoes?   _____

4. By the end of what month did Beth pick 35 tomatoes?   _____

5. Between the end of which two months did Beth pick the most
   tomatoes?   _____

6. Between the end of which two months did Beth pick the
   fewest tomatoes?   _____

7. Beth gave her aunt 22 of the tomatoes she picked and saved
   the rest for herself. How many tomatoes did Beth save for
   herself?   _____ tomatoes

8. Of the tomatoes Beth kept for herself, she canned 14 of them
   to use over the winter months. How many tomatoes did Beth
   have left after canning 14 of them?   _____ tomatoes

9. From the end of May to the end of July, how many tomatoes
   did Beth pick?   _____ tomatoes

CHAPTER 17

Lesson 3 Line Graphs

Use the line graph below to answer each question.

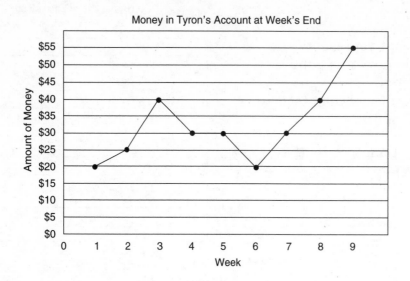

1. How much money did Tyron have at the end of week 4? $ _____

2. How much money did Tyron have at the end of week 6? $ _____

3. How much money did Tyron have at the end of week 9? $ _____

4. At the end of which week(s) did Tyron first have $25?   _____

5. At the end of which week(s) did Tyron have $40?   _____

6. At the end of how many weeks did Tyron have $30?   _____

7. Did the amount of money in Tyron's account increase,
   decrease, or stay the same between the end of week 3 and
   the end of week 4?   _____

8. Did the amount of money in Tyron's account increase,
   decrease, or stay the same between the end of week 4 and
   the end of week 5?   _____

9. By how much did Tyron's account increase between the
   end of week 8 and the end of week 9? $ _____

10. By how much did Tyron's account decrease between the
    end of week 5 and the end of week 6? $ _____

Lesson 4 Probability

Probability is the chance that an event will happen.

In the spinner to the right, spinning to a dotted section has a probability of $\frac{1}{4}$. The numerator is 1 because there is one dotted section of the spinner. The denominator is 4 because there are four sections of the spinner.

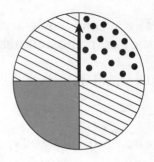

Ring the correct probability for the spinner to the right.

1. The probability of spinning to a striped section is

$\frac{1}{5}$ $\qquad$ $\frac{3}{5}$ $\qquad$ $\frac{2}{5}$

2. The probability of spinning to a solid section is

$\frac{3}{5}$ $\qquad$ $\frac{2}{5}$ $\qquad$ $\frac{1}{5}$

3. The probability of spinning to a dotted section is

$\frac{1}{5}$ $\qquad$ $\frac{2}{5}$ $\qquad$ $\frac{3}{5}$

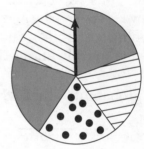

Ring the correct probability for the spinner to the right.

4. The probability of spinning to a 2 is

$\frac{1}{6}$ $\qquad$ $\frac{2}{6}$ $\qquad$ $\frac{3}{6}$

5. The probability of spinning to a 6 is

$\frac{3}{6}$ $\qquad$ $\frac{1}{6}$ $\qquad$ $\frac{2}{6}$

6. The probability of spinning to a 1 is

$\frac{2}{6}$ $\qquad$ $\frac{3}{6}$ $\qquad$ $\frac{1}{6}$

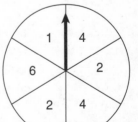

Lesson 4 Problem Solving

Complete each probability.

1. Taylor and Josh are playing a game. Each turn they spin the spinner shown to the right.

   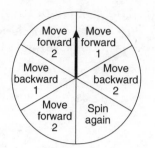

   The probability of spinning "move forward 2" is _____.

   The probability of spinning "spin again" is _____.

   The probability of spinning "move backward 1" is _____.

2. Susana has a bag with ten marbles. There are two red marbles, three blue marbles, and five yellow marbles. Susana closes her eyes and picks one marble out of the bag.

   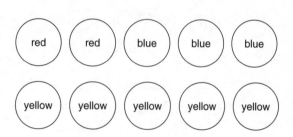

   The probability that Susana will pick a blue marble is _____.

   The probability that Susana will pick a red marble is _____.

   The probability that Susana will pick a yellow marble is _____.

CHAPTER 17 PRACTICE TEST
Graphs and Probability

Use the bar graph to answer each question.

1. How many students chose lemonade as their favorite beverage? _____ students

2. How many students chose fruit juice as their favorite beverage? _____ students

3. What beverage did 25 students choose as their favorite? _____

4. What beverage did 60 students choose as their favorite? _____

5. How many more students chose soda as their favorite beverage than milk? _____ students

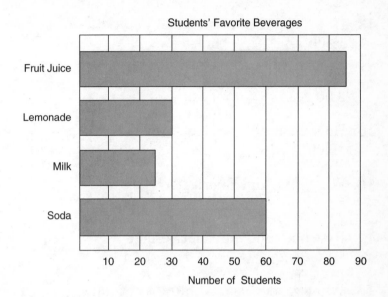

Students' Favorite Beverages

6. How many total students chose fruit juice or lemonade as their favorite beverage? _____ students

Use the picture graph to answer each question.

7. How many hoagies were sold on Sunday at the Pizzeria? _____

8. How many pizzas were sold Sunday at the Pizzeria? _____

9. The Pizzeria sold 45 _____ on Sunday?

10. The Pizzeria sold 30 _____ on Sunday?

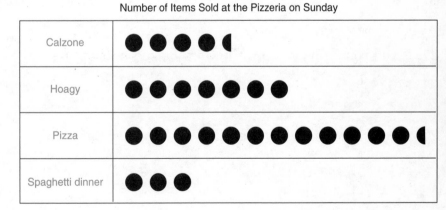

Number of Items Sold at the Pizzeria on Sunday

Key: ● = 10 items

11. How many more pizzas than hoagies were sold on Sunday? _____

12. If the Pizzeria sold 60 ravioli dinners on Sunday, how many symbols would there be for ravioli dinners? _____ symbols

CHAPTER 17

CHAPTER 17 PRACTICE TEST (continued)

Use the line graph to answer each question.

13. How far did Cherise bike by 11:00 A.M.? _____ miles

14. How far did Cherise bike by 2:00 P.M.? _____ miles

15. How far did Cherise bike by 12:00 P.M.? _____ miles

16. What time did Cherise start her bike ride? _____

17. By what time did Cherise bike 10 miles? _____

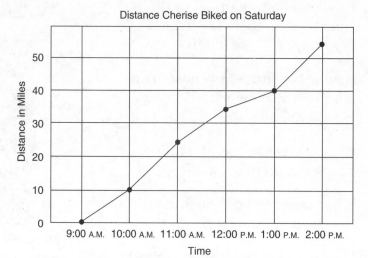

Distance Cherise Biked on Saturday

18. What is the greatest number of miles that Cherise biked in one hour? _____ miles

19. What is the least number of miles that Cherise biked in one hour? _____ miles

Ring the correct probability for the spinner.

20. The probability of spinning to a solid section is

$\frac{3}{5}$ $\qquad$ $\frac{2}{5}$ $\qquad$ $\frac{1}{5}$

21. The probability of spinning to a dotted section is

$\frac{1}{5}$ $\qquad$ $\frac{3}{5}$ $\qquad$ $\frac{2}{5}$

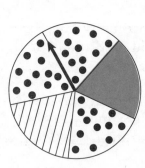

22. The probability of spinning to a striped section is

$\frac{1}{5}$ $\qquad$ $\frac{2}{5}$ $\qquad$ $\frac{3}{5}$

MID-TEST 1 Chapters 1-7

Add or subtract.

	a	*b*	*c*	*d*	*e*

1.
$$\begin{array}{r} 6 \\ +5 \\ \hline \end{array}$$
$$\begin{array}{r} 9 \\ +9 \\ \hline \end{array}$$
$$\begin{array}{r} 6\,1 \\ +5 \\ \hline \end{array}$$
$$\begin{array}{r} 3\,5 \\ +4\,3 \\ \hline \end{array}$$
$$\begin{array}{r} 9 \\ +4\,2 \\ \hline \end{array}$$

2.
$$\begin{array}{r} 8\,4 \\ +7 \\ \hline \end{array}$$
$$\begin{array}{r} 6\,4 \\ +1\,8 \\ \hline \end{array}$$
$$\begin{array}{r} 7\,0 \\ +7\,0 \\ \hline \end{array}$$
$$\begin{array}{r} 1\,8 \\ +9\,3 \\ \hline \end{array}$$
$$\begin{array}{r} 8\,5 \\ +8\,9 \\ \hline \end{array}$$

3.
$$\begin{array}{r} 7\,0 \\ 8\,0 \\ +3\,0 \\ \hline \end{array}$$
$$\begin{array}{r} 4\,7\,8 \\ +5\,9\,6 \\ \hline \end{array}$$
$$\begin{array}{r} 2\,5\,6 \\ 1\,7\,5 \\ +3\,1\,0 \\ \hline \end{array}$$
$$\begin{array}{r} \$6.9\,8 \\ +7.2\,3 \\ \hline \end{array}$$
$$\begin{array}{r} \$1\,1.6\,2 \\ 3.6\,5 \\ +1.9\,8 \\ \hline \end{array}$$

4.
$$\begin{array}{r} 1\,6 \\ -7 \\ \hline \end{array}$$
$$\begin{array}{r} 1\,5 \\ -6 \\ \hline \end{array}$$
$$\begin{array}{r} 3\,8 \\ -4 \\ \hline \end{array}$$
$$\begin{array}{r} 8\,7 \\ -1\,5 \\ \hline \end{array}$$
$$\begin{array}{r} 5\,6 \\ -8 \\ \hline \end{array}$$

5.
$$\begin{array}{r} 4\,3 \\ -7 \\ \hline \end{array}$$
$$\begin{array}{r} 8\,0 \\ -1\,7 \\ \hline \end{array}$$
$$\begin{array}{r} 1\,5\,0 \\ -7\,0 \\ \hline \end{array}$$
$$\begin{array}{r} 1\,3\,6 \\ -6\,9 \\ \hline \end{array}$$
$$\begin{array}{r} 1\,8\,1 \\ -9\,3 \\ \hline \end{array}$$

6.
$$\begin{array}{r} 8\,7\,6 \\ -9\,7 \\ \hline \end{array}$$
$$\begin{array}{r} 6\,2\,5 \\ -2\,0\,8 \\ \hline \end{array}$$
$$\begin{array}{r} 8\,7\,2\,4 \\ -8\,9\,3 \\ \hline \end{array}$$
$$\begin{array}{r} \$9.8\,5 \\ -6.2\,7 \\ \hline \end{array}$$
$$\begin{array}{r} \$1\,8.2\,0 \\ -6.7\,5 \\ \hline \end{array}$$

For each clockface, write the numerals that name the time.

7.

a	*b*	*c*

_____ : _____   _____ : _____   _____ : _____

Compare each pair of numbers. Write < or >.

	a	b	c	d
8.	18_____13	9_____11	34_____37	83_____39
9.	7_____3	19_____9	44_____53	64_____60

Round each number to the place named.

	a	b	c
10.	967: tens _____	4,826: hundreds _____	7,186: thousands _____
11.	87: tens _____	561: hundreds _____	3,706: thousands _____

Solve each problem.

12. There are nine bolts in one package. There are six bolts in another package. How many bolts are in both packages?

There are _____ bolts in both packages.

13. There are 27 letters to be typed. Only 6 letters have been typed. How many letters still need to be typed?

_____ letters still need to be typed.

14. Dirk read 84 pages in the morning. He read 69 pages in the afternoon. How many pages did he read that day?

He read _____ pages that day.

15. You bought items at a store that cost $1.45, $2.98, and $9.98. How much did these items cost in all?

These items cost $_____ in all.

16. Jennifer wants to buy a purse that costs $18.29. She has $9.55. How much more does she need to buy the purse?

She needs $_____ more.

12.	13.
14.	**15.**
16.	

STOP

MID-TEST 2   Chapters 1–12

Add or subtract.

	a	*b*	*c*	*d*	*e*
1.	7 +8	6 5 +3	8 2 +1 6	2 6 +9	7 3 +1 9
2.	2 0 +9 0	6 9 +4 3	1 6 5 +9 2 7	3 6 7 2 +3 5	$2 1.4 3 +6 2.9 7
3.	1 2 −4	5 6 −5	9 3 −8 3	6 2 −7	8 5 −4 7
4.	1 8 0 −9 0	1 2 5 −7 6	7 8 0 −5 3 9	3 7 5 1 −8 6 5	$2 5.0 0 −7.2 5

Which digit is in the place named?

	a	*b*

5. 279: tens   3,079: hundreds

_____ is in the tens place.   _____ is in the hundreds place.

6. 861: ones   5,472: thousands

_____ is in the ones place.   _____ is in the thousands place.

Ring all even numbers.

7.   6   9   11   18   33   45   52   76   80   93   127   144

Ring all odd numbers.

8.   1   3   8   12   18   27   40   55   66   82   91   109

GO

Multiply.

	a	*b*	*c*	*d*	*e*
9.	5 ×3	4 ×4	6 ×5	8 ×3	7 ×2
10.	3 ×9	8 ×7	6 ×8	9 ×7	6 ×6

Multiply.

	a	*b*	*c*	*d*
11.	7 0 ×5	2 3 ×3	1 8 ×7	4 3 ×7
12.	3 9 ×2	1 5 ×4	6 1 ×5	5 3 ×6

Divide.

13. 2)1 2   4)2 0   3)2 7   1)8

14. 5)4 0   4)2 4   7)0   8)7 2

15. 9)3 6   7)4 9   6)4 8   9)5 4

GO

MID-TEST 2   Chapters 1–12 (continued)

Answer each question. Use the calendar to help you.

June						
S	**M**	**T**	**W**	**T**	**F**	**S**
				1	2	3
4	5	6	7	8	9	10
11	12	13	14	15	16	17
18	19	20	21	22	23	24
25	26	27	28	29	30	

16. How many days are in June? _____

17. On what day is June 17? _____

18. Write the numerals that name the time.

_____ : _____

Write a Roman numeral for each of the following.

	a	*b*	*c*
19.	4 = _____	8 = _____	12 = _____
20.	17 = _____	25 = _____	33 = _____
21.	9 = _____	28 = _____	19 = _____

Add or subtract.

	a	*b*	*c*	*d*
22.	$0.2 3 +0.5 9	$4.1 5 +3.6 2	$3.0 9 +9.8 3	$8.7 6 +1 5.3 3
23.	$4.4 9 −1.2 8	$1 1.6 4 −7.1 6	$6.0 0 −2.7 6	$3 7.0 6 −1 9.5 5
24.	$3 5.0 0 −1 7.0 3	$8 5.4 0 −5 6.7 4	$5 0.5 5 −1 8.2 9	$9 7.1 3 −9 3.7 2

Solve each problem.

25. Amanda worked in the automobile factory for 45 days. She worked 5 days each week. How many weeks did she work?

Amanda worked _____ weeks.

26. One store sold 421 radios. Another store sold 294 radios. A third store sold 730 radios. How many radios did all three stores sell?

All three stores sold _____ radios.

27. Ms. O'Connor received 1,439 votes. Mr. Ortega received 810 votes. How many more votes did Ms. O'Connor receive than Mr. Ortega?

Ms. O'Connor received _____ more votes.

28. Branden bought 24 liters of paint. The paint was in 6 cans. All the cans were the same size. How many liters of paint were in each can?

There were _____ liters of paint in each can.

29. A farmer has 6 stacks of bales of hay. Each stack has 36 bales. How many bales of hay does the farmer have?

The farmer has _____ bales of hay.

30. Larysa bought items that cost $3.80, $2.29, and $1.75. The sales tax was $0.47. How much did she pay for those items, including tax?

She paid $_____.

31. Don had $27.89. He spent $11.92. How much did he have left?

Don had $_____ left.

25.

26.

27.

28.

29.

30.

31.

STOP

FINAL TEST   Chapters 1-17

Add.

	a	b	c	d	e
1.	6 +5	9 +7	3 6 +2	5 6 +2 3	7 +5 5
2.	2 9 +4 6	6 0 +2 8	9 8 +1 6	2 1 8 +6 4 0	3 5 4 +7 8 5
3.	1 5 4 +3 0	6 4 9 8 +5 6	3 7 1 9 +7 9	6 7 5 4 3 2 +1 0 9	5 8 7 6 0 5 +9 3 2

Subtract.

	a	b	c	d	e
4.	1 3 −6	1 6 −7	4 6 −3	5 9 −8	6 5 −3 2
5.	3 5 −7	8 5 −7 1	6 3 −1 8	1 6 4 −8 1	1 4 6 −7 8
6.	7 8 9 −3 6 2	6 4 1 −1 9 7	3 8 0 −2 0 7	1 7 0 8 −4 8 5	8 3 5 7 −6 2 4

Which digit is in the place named?

	a	*b*
7.	615: ones	904: hundreds
	_____ is in the ones place.	_____ is in the hundreds place.
8.	4,635: thousands	1,089: tens
	_____ is in the thousands place.	_____ is in the tens place.

Compare each pair of numbers. Write < or >.

	a	*b*	*c*	*d*
9.	9 _____ 7	15 _____ 12	22 _____ 32	57 _____ 60
10.	17 _____ 19	37 _____ 35	63 _____ 64	80 _____ 83

Ring all even numbers.

11. 14 3 6 10 21 33 0 20 37 44 75 93 100

Ring all odd numbers.

12. 13 4 5 12 25 46 7 39 42 60 81 88 104

Round each number to the place named.

	a	*b*	*c*
13.	167: hundreds _____	928: tens _____	4,687: thousands _____
14.	7,271: tens _____	629: hundreds _____	5,114: thousands _____

Estimate each sum or difference.

	a	*b*	*c*	*d*	*e*
15.	38 +12	93 +65	56 +32	297 +845	126 +781
16.	76 −34	55 −19	237 −44	537 −156	871 −348
17.	416 +357	973 +542	6417 −386	1473 −925	7048 −3607

GO ▶

Use the calendar to answer each question.

18. How many days are in March? _____

19. How many Mondays are in March? _____

20. How many Thursdays are in March? _____

21. What date is the second Tuesday in March? _____

22. On what day is March 18? _____

23. On what day is March 30? _____

March						
S	**M**	**T**	**W**	**T**	**F**	**S**
				1	2	3
4	5	6	7	8	9	10
11	12	13	14	15	16	17
18	19	20	21	22	23	24
25	26	27	28	29	30	31

Write the time for each clockface.

a	b	c	d

24.

_____ : _____   _____ : _____   _____ : _____   _____ : _____

Write the number for each Roman numeral.

a	b	c	d

25. V = _____   VII = _____   XIV = _____   XXIII = _____

26. XVII = _____   XXX = _____   XXVII = _____   XXXV = _____

Add or subtract.

a	b	c	d

27.
$$\begin{array}{r} \$3.1\,7 \\ +1.9\,5 \\ \hline \end{array} \qquad \begin{array}{r} \$8.4\,5 \\ +6.2\,3 \\ \hline \end{array} \qquad \begin{array}{r} \$1\,5.3\,7 \\ +\ \ 8.9\,9 \\ \hline \end{array} \qquad \begin{array}{r} \$2\,7.9\,5 \\ +3\,4.1\,8 \\ \hline \end{array}$$

28.
$$\begin{array}{r} \$3.6\,4 \\ -1.7\,2 \\ \hline \end{array} \qquad \begin{array}{r} \$1\,4.2\,8 \\ -\ \ 5.9\,5 \\ \hline \end{array} \qquad \begin{array}{r} \$2\,5.0\,0 \\ -2\,1.7\,6 \\ \hline \end{array} \qquad \begin{array}{r} \$4\,3.5\,7 \\ -2\,0.6\,1 \\ \hline \end{array}$$

SPECTRUM MATHEMATICS
Red Book

FINAL TEST
CH. 1–17

GO

FINAL TEST
Chapters 1-17

223

Multiply.

	a	*b*	*c*	*d*
29.	4 ×2	3 ×7	8 ×6	0 ×5
30.	5 ×3	8 ×1	9 ×8	8 ×7
31.	4 0 ×3	3 5 ×7	3 9 ×2	6 0 ×5
32.	5 1 ×6	4 5 ×9	1 6 ×2	4 4 ×4

Divide.

	a	*b*	*c*	*d*
33.	3)6	2)8	1)7	3)9
34.	2)1 6	3)2 7	5)2 0	3)2 4
35.	6)3 0	8)5 6	7)2 8	6)5 4
36.	9)2 7	7)6 3	9)0	8)4 0

GO

FINAL TEST Chapters 1–17 (continued)

Find each length to the nearest centimeter.

37. _____ centimeters ▬▬▬▬▬▬▬

38. _____ centimeters ▬▬▬▬▬▬▬▬▬▬▬

Find the length to the nearest inch.

39. _____ inches ▬▬▬▬▬▬▬▬▬

40. _____ inches ▬▬▬▬▬▬▬▬▬▬▬▬▬

What is the temperature reading on each thermometer?

| *a* | *b* | *c* |

41.

 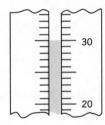

_____ °F   _____ °F   _____ °F

What fraction of each circle is shaded?

| *a* | *b* | *c* |

42.

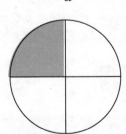 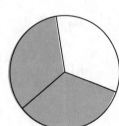 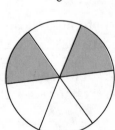

_____   _____   _____

FINAL TEST
CH. 1–17

GO ▶

FINAL TEST
Chapters 1–17

225

Name each figure shown.

	a	*b*	*c*

43.

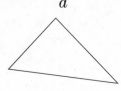  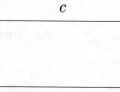

_____ _____ _____

44.

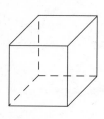 

_____ _____ _____

Find the perimeter of each figure.

	a	*b*	*c*

45.

13 inches   8 inches
14 inches

4 cm
6 cm   6 cm
8 cm

17 ft
9 ft   9 ft
17 ft

_____ inches   _____ centimeters   _____ feet

Use the bar graph to answer each question.

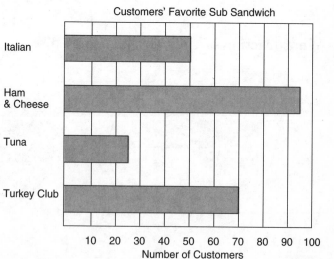

Customers' Favorite Sub Sandwich

46. How many customers chose a tuna sub as their favorite? _____ customers

47. How many customers chose an Italian sub as their favorite? _____ customers

48. What type of sub sandwich did 70 customers choose as their favorite?
_____

49. How many more customers chose a ham and cheese sub as their favorite sub sandwich than an Italian sub? _____ customers

STOP

CHAPTER 1 CUMULATIVE REVIEW

Work each problem.
Find the correct answer.
Mark the space for the answer.

Part 1 Concepts

1. To check 7 + 8 = 15, subtract 8 from ____.

A 8   C 7
B 15   D 10

2. To check 10 − 7 = 3, add ____ to 7.

F 4   H 3
G 10   J 7

Part 2 Computation

3. 3
      +9

A 10
B 6
C 12
D 15

4. 1 4
      −6

F 8
G 10
H 7
J 20

5. 1 3
      −8

A 5
B 4
C 7
D 3

6. 8
      +6

F 10
G 13
H 14
J 15

Part 3 Applications

7. Kelly ran 3 miles yesterday. She ran 5 miles today. How many miles did she run in all?

A 2   C 7
B 8   D 10

8. Jamaal is 13 years old. His sister is 9 years old. How many years older is Jamaal than his sister?

F 4   H 22
G 3   J 6

9. Ten bolts and nuts were on the table. Five were bolts. How many were nuts?

A 5   C 4
B 10   D 0

10. Shauna wants to collect 15 dolls. She has 7 dolls. How many more dolls does she need?

F 6   H 7
G 4   J 8

ANSWER ROW   **1** Ⓐ Ⓑ © Ⓓ   **3** Ⓐ Ⓑ © Ⓓ   **5** Ⓐ Ⓑ © Ⓓ   **7** Ⓐ Ⓑ © Ⓓ   **9** Ⓐ Ⓑ © Ⓓ
2 Ⓕ Ⓖ Ⓗ Ⓙ   **4** Ⓕ Ⓖ Ⓗ Ⓙ   **6** Ⓕ Ⓖ Ⓗ Ⓙ   **8** Ⓕ Ⓖ Ⓗ Ⓙ   **10** Ⓕ Ⓖ Ⓗ Ⓙ

SPECTRUM MATHEMATICS
Red Book

CHAPTER 1
CUMULATIVE REVIEW
227

NAME _____

Work each problem.
Find the correct answer.
Mark the space for the answer.

Part 1 Concepts

1. Which number is in the ones place in 563?

A 5   C 3
B 6   D 1

2. Which number is in the tens place in 6,318?

F 6   H 1
G 3   J 8

Part 2 Computation

3.   4
    +9

A 10
B 13
C 12
D 15

4. 100 + 3 =

F 300
G 301
H 130
J 103

5. 600 + 70 + 9 =

A 6,709
B 609
C 769
D 679

6.   5
    +8

F 11
G 3
H 13
J 10

Part 3 Applications

7. Vinny lives four blocks from school. Randy lives six blocks from school. Alexis lives two blocks from school. John lives five blocks from school. Who lives the farthest from school?

A Vinny   C Alexis
B Randy   D John

8. Sarah collects stamps. At the end of one year, she had 462 stamps. To the nearest tens, how many stamps does Sarah have?

F 460   H 400
G 560   J 500

9. Jeff rode his bike 5 miles. Carmen rode her bike 3 miles. Tia rode her bike 4 miles. Davon rode his bike 6 miles. Who rode the most miles?

A Jeff   C Tia
B Davon   D Carmen

10. Mrs. Ferrel spent $237 at the grocery store. How much did she spend rounded to the nearest ten?

F $230   H $240
G $200   J $300

ANSWER ROW **1** Ⓐ Ⓑ Ⓒ Ⓓ   **3** Ⓐ Ⓑ Ⓒ Ⓓ   **5** Ⓐ Ⓑ Ⓒ Ⓓ   **7** Ⓐ Ⓑ Ⓒ Ⓓ   **9** Ⓐ Ⓑ Ⓒ Ⓓ
            2 Ⓕ Ⓖ Ⓗ Ⓙ   **4** Ⓕ Ⓖ Ⓗ Ⓙ   **6** Ⓕ Ⓖ Ⓗ Ⓙ   **8** Ⓕ Ⓖ Ⓗ Ⓙ   **10** Ⓕ Ⓖ Ⓗ Ⓙ

CHAPTER 3 CUMULATIVE REVIEW

Work each problem.
Find the correct answer.
Mark the space for the answer.

Part 1 Concepts

1. The sum of 39 and 64 is closest to _____.

   A 70
   B 80
   C 90
   D 100

2. Which of the following inequalities is correct?

   F $15 < 13$
   G $27 < 37$
   H $34 > 36$
   J $56 > 65$

3. 8,572 rounded to the nearest thousand is

   A 8,000   C 9,000
   B 8,600   D 8,570

Part 2 Computation

4. $\begin{array}{r} 15 \\ -11 \\ \hline \end{array}$

   F 26
   G 5
   H 7
   J 4

5. $\begin{array}{r} 51 \\ +23 \\ \hline \end{array}$

   A 54
   B 74
   C 28
   D 63

6. $\begin{array}{r} 84 \\ -30 \\ \hline \end{array}$

   F 114
   G 50
   H 54
   J 84

Part 3 Applications

7. Yesterday Kiah collected eight seashells. Today she collected nine seashells. How many seashells did Kiah collect in all?

   A 16   C 1
   B 17   D 13

8. Lin bought a used car for $7,635. How much did Lin pay for the car rounded to the nearest hundred?

   F $7,600   H $8,000
   G $7,500   J $7,640

9. On Friday Mr. Brown drove 57 miles. On Saturday he drove 33 miles. How many more miles did Mr. Brown drive on Friday?

   A 14   C 22
   B 90   D 24

10. Last month Kim worked 42 hours. This month she worked 57 hours. How many hours did Kim work in all?

   F 87   H 99
   G 15   J 79

CUMULATIVE REVIEW

ANSWER ROW **1** Ⓐ Ⓑ Ⓒ Ⓓ **3** Ⓐ Ⓑ Ⓒ Ⓓ **5** Ⓐ Ⓑ Ⓒ Ⓓ **7** Ⓐ Ⓑ Ⓒ Ⓓ **9** Ⓐ Ⓑ Ⓒ Ⓓ
　　　　　　　2 Ⓕ Ⓖ Ⓗ Ⓙ **4** Ⓕ Ⓖ Ⓗ Ⓙ **6** Ⓕ Ⓖ Ⓗ Ⓙ **8** Ⓕ Ⓖ Ⓗ Ⓙ **10** Ⓕ Ⓖ Ⓗ Ⓙ

Work each problem.
Find the correct answer.
Mark the space for the answer.

Part 1 Concepts

1. Which of these numbers is not even?

A 4

B 5

C 14

D 50

2. What digit is in the ones place in the sum 36 + 18?

F 5

G 6

H 2

J 4

3. 2,372 rounded to the nearest hundred is

A 2,000   C 2,400

B 2,300   D 2,370

Part 2 Computation

4. 1 1
$\underline{-6}$

F 5

G 4

H 7

J 17

5. 5 1
$\underline{-8}$

A 59

B 45

C 52

D 43

6.   5 7
     2 5
     4 3
$\underline{+8 6}$

F 211

G 207

H 191

J 217

Part 3 Applications

7. Suzie planted 15 sunflower seeds. Only 7 of them grew. How many seeds did not grow?

A 22   C 8

B 9   D 11

8. On Saturday Otis delivered 56 flowers. On Sunday he delivered 39 flowers. How many more flowers did Otis deliver on Saturday?

F 27   H 95

G 17   J 14

9. There are 463 students at Ridge Elementary School. How many students are there? Round to the nearest hundred.

A 400   C 500

B 460   D 470

10. On the first math test Maggie answered 26 questions correctly. On the second math test Maggie answered 32 questions correctly. How many more questions did Maggie answer correctly on the second test?

F 8   H 10

G 4   J 6

ANSWER ROW   **1** Ⓐ Ⓑ Ⓒ Ⓓ   **3** Ⓐ Ⓑ Ⓒ Ⓓ   **5** Ⓐ Ⓑ Ⓒ Ⓓ   **7** Ⓐ Ⓑ Ⓒ Ⓓ   **9** Ⓐ Ⓑ Ⓒ Ⓓ

           2 Ⓕ Ⓖ Ⓗ Ⓙ   **4** Ⓕ Ⓖ Ⓗ Ⓙ   **6** Ⓕ Ⓖ Ⓗ Ⓙ   **8** Ⓕ Ⓖ Ⓗ Ⓙ   **10** Ⓕ Ⓖ Ⓗ Ⓙ

SPECTRUM MATHEMATICS
Red Book

230

CHAPTER 4
CUMULATIVE REVIEW

NAME _____

Work each problem.
Find the correct answer.
Mark the space for the answer.

Part 1 Concepts

1. The sum of 72 and 85 is closest to

A 10
B 130
C 160
D 200

2. How many of these numbers are greater than 83?

| 79 84 102 81 80 88 |

F 5
G 4
H 3
J 2

Part 2 Computation

3.   3 9
      +3 5

A 76
B 4
C 64
D 74

4.   9 5
      −7 1

F 44
G 24
H 45
J 50

5.   9 4
      +9 8

A 192
B 124
C 208
D 292

6. 1 3 2
     −9 4

F 48
G 230
H 38
J 34

Part 3 Applications

7. Jordan has 53 trading cards. Leon has 77 trading cards. How many trading cards do they have together?

A 120   C 24
B 130   D 128

8. Mr. Tung flew 448 miles on a business trip. How many miles did he fly? Round to the nearest ten.

F 450   H 500
G 400   J 440

9. There were three sections on the science test. Elisa scored 33 on one section and 35 on the second section. What was Elisa's total score on the test?

A 2   C 68
B 62   D 8

10. There are 134 third-grade students at Middletown School. There are 78 boys. How many girls are there?

F 56   H 78
G 66   J 54

CUMULATIVE REVIEW

ANSWER ROW   **1** Ⓐ Ⓑ Ⓒ Ⓓ   **3** Ⓐ Ⓑ Ⓒ Ⓓ   **5** Ⓐ Ⓑ Ⓒ Ⓓ   **7** Ⓐ Ⓑ Ⓒ Ⓓ   **9** Ⓐ Ⓑ Ⓒ Ⓓ
             2 Ⓕ Ⓖ Ⓗ Ⓙ   **4** Ⓕ Ⓖ Ⓗ Ⓙ   **6** Ⓕ Ⓖ Ⓗ Ⓙ   **8** Ⓕ Ⓖ Ⓗ Ⓙ   **10** Ⓕ Ⓖ Ⓗ Ⓙ

NAME _____

Work each problem.
Find the correct answer.
Mark the space for the answer.

Part 1 Concepts

1. How many tens are in 62?

   A 2

   B 6

   C 10

   D 62

2. What is the estimated sum of 486 + 741?

   F 1,300

   G 1,100

   H 1,000

   J 1,200

Part 2 Computation

3.   9
  +9

   A 10

   B 16

   C 18

   D 20

4.   9 8 1
 −8 6 1

   F 120

   G 115

   H 122

   J 90

5.   5 6 2
 +7 4 9

   A 1,201

   B 1,311

   C 187

   D 1,362

6. 7 5 3 4
  −2 7 8

   F 7,256

   G 7,364

   H 6,936

   J 7,812

Part 3 Applications

7. Heather bought a pack of 36 balloons. She also bought a pack of 15 jumbo balloons. How many balloons did Heather buy in all?

   A 21   C 41

   B 51   D 53

8. There are 67 days until Tanya's birthday, 125 days until Alvin's birthday, 80 days until David's birthday, and 119 days until Max's birthday. Whose birthday is the furthest away?

   F Tanya   H Alvin

   G David   J Max

9. Last month Paco spent 36 hours mowing lawns. This month he spent 57 hours mowing lawns. What is the estimated number of hours that Paco spent mowing lawns in all?

   A 90   C 120

   B 20   D 100

10. Last month, Jason bought four cases of baseball cards holding the following amounts: 675, 593, 607, and 753. How many baseball cards did Jason buy last month?

   F 1,268   H 2,658

   G 2,628   J 2,358

ANSWER ROW **1** Ⓐ Ⓑ Ⓒ Ⓓ **3** Ⓐ Ⓑ Ⓒ Ⓓ **5** Ⓐ Ⓑ Ⓒ Ⓓ **7** Ⓐ Ⓑ Ⓒ Ⓓ **9** Ⓐ Ⓑ Ⓒ Ⓓ

             2 Ⓕ Ⓖ Ⓗ Ⓙ **4** Ⓕ Ⓖ Ⓗ Ⓙ **6** Ⓕ Ⓖ Ⓗ Ⓙ **8** Ⓕ Ⓖ Ⓗ Ⓙ **10** Ⓕ Ⓖ Ⓗ Ⓙ

Work each problem.
Find the correct answer.
Mark the space for the answer.

Part 1 Concepts

1. Which row has all even numbers?

A 0, 8, 21, 36

B 2, 9, 20, 44

C 5, 10, 28, 32

D 6, 12, 38, 50

2. What number is represented by the Roman numeral XXIV?

F 34

G 24

H 26

J 14

3. 39 = _____

A XXXXI

B XXVVIII

C XXXVIII

D XXXIX

Part 2 Computation

4. 1 4 0
  − 9 0

F 50

G 40

H 230

J 60

5.   5 1 6
   7 0 9
   8 2 3
  +6 7 4

A 2,718

B 2,692

C 2,722

D 2,935

6.   6 3
  +2 6

F 89

G 37

H 98

J 83

Part 3 Applications

7. Marshall waited in line 48 minutes to ride the roller coaster. Byron waited in line 29 minutes to ride the roller coaster. How many more minutes did Marshall wait in line than Byron?

A 21   C 19

B 77   D 29

8. Mrs. Jenkins is 42 years old. Her son is 15 years old. How many years older is Mrs. Jenkins than her son?

F 37   H 27

G 57   J 25

9. Patty has $257 in her savings account. Felicia has $1,025 in her savings account. How much more money does Felicia have in her account than Patty?

A $768   C $1,282

B $868   D $752

10. The XXVI Olympic games were in Atlanta, Georgia. What number were these Olympic games?

F 14   H 24

G 26   J 36

ANSWER ROW   **1** Ⓐ Ⓑ Ⓒ Ⓓ   **3** Ⓐ Ⓑ Ⓒ Ⓓ   **5** Ⓐ Ⓑ Ⓒ Ⓓ   **7** Ⓐ Ⓑ Ⓒ Ⓓ   **9** Ⓐ Ⓑ Ⓒ Ⓓ

2 Ⓕ Ⓖ Ⓗ Ⓙ   **4** Ⓕ Ⓖ Ⓗ Ⓙ   **6** Ⓕ Ⓖ Ⓗ Ⓙ   **8** Ⓕ Ⓖ Ⓗ Ⓙ   **10** Ⓕ Ⓖ Ⓗ Ⓙ

CUMULATIVE REVIEW

NAME _____

Work each problem.
Find the correct answer.
Mark the space for the answer.

Part 1 Concepts

1. What number is missing from the sequence below?

   3, 8, 13, 18, 23, 28, _____

   A 25
   B 33
   C 15
   D 29

2. $9 + 9 + 9 + 9 + 9$ means
   F $5 + 9$.
   G 9×9.
   H 5×9.
   J $4 + 9$.

Part 2 Computation

3. $\begin{array}{r} 7\,5 \\ -2\,6 \\ \hline \end{array}$

   A 39
   B 59
   C 101
   D 49

4. $\begin{array}{r} 5\,0 \\ 7\,5 \\ +2\,4 \\ \hline \end{array}$

   F 125
   G 149
   H 135
   J 99

5. $\begin{array}{r} \$9.67 \\ +0.32 \\ \hline \end{array}$

   A $9.89
   B $9.35
   C $9.99
   D $10.99

6. $\begin{array}{r} 2 \\ \times 8 \\ \hline \end{array}$

   F 16
   G 10
   H 24
   J 14

Part 3 Applications

7. Last week Mr. Turner worked 35 hours. This week he worked 44 hours. How many hours did Mr. Turner work in all?

   A 89   C 75
   B 79   D 9

8. There are two buses taking 124 students on a field trip. There are 67 students on one bus. How many students are on the other bus?

   F 63   H 61
   G 57   J 71

9. Randy spent $534 on a new guitar. How much did he spend? Round to the nearest hundred.

   A $400   C $530
   B $600   D $500

10. Alexandria can ride her bicycle 4 miles in one hour. How far can she ride in three hours?

    F 12 miles   H 9 miles
    G 7 miles   J 14 miles

ANSWER ROW   1 Ⓐ Ⓑ Ⓒ Ⓓ   3 Ⓐ Ⓑ Ⓒ Ⓓ   5 Ⓐ Ⓑ Ⓒ Ⓓ   7 Ⓐ Ⓑ Ⓒ Ⓓ   9 Ⓐ Ⓑ Ⓒ Ⓓ
             2 Ⓕ Ⓖ Ⓗ Ⓙ   4 Ⓕ Ⓖ Ⓗ Ⓙ   6 Ⓕ Ⓖ Ⓗ Ⓙ   8 Ⓕ Ⓖ Ⓗ Ⓙ   10 Ⓕ Ⓖ Ⓗ Ⓙ

NAME _____

Work each problem.
Find the correct answer.
Mark the space for the answer.

Part 1 Concepts

1. Which number has a 7 in the hundreds place?

   A 5,437
   B 6,570
   C 7,032
   D 1,795

2. Which number is less than 32?

   F 131
   G 29
   H 38
   J 33

Part 2 Computation

3. 27
   +39

   A 66
   B 68
   C 56
   D 57

4. 72¢
   −27¢

   F 54¢
   G 55¢
   H 45¢
   J 99¢

5. 5
   ×6

   A 11
   B 35
   C 42
   D 30

6. 8
   ×8

   F 16
   G 64
   H 56
   J 48

Part 3 Applications

7. Brandon scored 15 points in the basketball game. Alex scored 11 points in the game. How many points did they score together?

   A 25   C 16
   B 26   D 4

8. Joseph has saved $57.25 to buy a bicycle. The bicycle costs $95.75. How much more money does Joseph need to buy the bicycle?

   F $38.50   H $48.50
   G $153.00   J $35.75

9. A machine produces 4,518 parts each day. One day 276 of the parts were defective. How many of the parts were not defective that day?

   A 3,982   C 4,794
   B 4,242   D 4,352

10. Mina works four days a week. She works nine hours each day. How many hours does Mina work each week?

    F 40   H 36
    G 13   J 32

CUMULATIVE REVIEW

ANSWER ROW   1 Ⓐ Ⓑ Ⓒ Ⓓ   3 Ⓐ Ⓑ Ⓒ Ⓓ   5 Ⓐ Ⓑ Ⓒ Ⓓ   7 Ⓐ Ⓑ Ⓒ Ⓓ   9 Ⓐ Ⓑ Ⓒ Ⓓ
             2 Ⓕ Ⓖ Ⓗ Ⓙ   4 Ⓕ Ⓖ Ⓗ Ⓙ   6 Ⓕ Ⓖ Ⓗ Ⓙ   8 Ⓕ Ⓖ Ⓗ Ⓙ   10 Ⓕ Ⓖ Ⓗ Ⓙ

SPECTRUM MATHEMATICS
Red Book

CHAPTER 9
CUMULATIVE REVIEW
235

Work each problem.
Find the correct answer.
Mark the space for the answer.

Part 1 Concepts

1. Which of the following numbers is odd?

A 36
B 67
C 52
D 90

2. XIV = _____

F 24
G 15
H 14
J 16

3. The sum of 23 + 9 is closest to

A 20
B 10
C 30
D 40

Part 2 Computation

4.   556
   374
 +897

F 1,617
G 1,453
H 930
J 1,827

5.   7
  ×7

A 14
B 49
C 42
D 36

6. 27
  ×8

F 216
G 35
H 208
J 166

Part 3 Applications

7. Tim read 47 pages on Monday. He read 25 pages on Tuesday. How many more pages did Tim read on Monday?

A 72   C 12
B 22   D 25

8. At lunch Jamie spent $3.75 on a sandwich and $0.90 on a soft drink. How much money did Jamie spend for lunch?

F $2.85   H $3.65
G $4.65   J $4.85

9. Marta babysat for four hours. She earns $6 per hour. How much money did Marta earn baby-sitting?

A $10   C $26
B $18   D $24

10. Mr. Garcia ordered seven buses for a field trip. There were 36 students on each bus. How many students were there in all on the field trip?

F 252   H 238
G 182   J 198

ANSWER ROW   **1** Ⓐ Ⓑ Ⓒ Ⓓ   **3** Ⓐ Ⓑ Ⓒ Ⓓ   **5** Ⓐ Ⓑ Ⓒ Ⓓ   **7** Ⓐ Ⓑ Ⓒ Ⓓ   **9** Ⓐ Ⓑ Ⓒ Ⓓ
                  2 Ⓕ Ⓖ Ⓗ Ⓙ   **4** Ⓕ Ⓖ Ⓗ Ⓙ   **6** Ⓕ Ⓖ Ⓗ Ⓙ   **8** Ⓕ Ⓖ Ⓗ Ⓙ   **10** Ⓕ Ⓖ Ⓗ Ⓙ

CHAPTER 11 CUMULATIVE REVIEW

Work each problem.
Find the correct answer.
Mark the space for the answer.

Part 1 Concepts

1. Another way to write 4×8 is

   A $4 + 4 + 4 + 4.$

   B $4 + 8.$

   C $8 + 8 + 8 + 8.$

   D $8 \times 8 \times 8 \times 8.$

2. $138 < $ _____

   F 135

   G 141

   H 129

   J 109

Part 2 Computation

3. $\begin{array}{r} 96 \\ -72 \end{array}$

    A 168

    B 34

    C 24

    D 28

4. $\begin{array}{r} 20 \\ 81 \\ +16 \end{array}$

    F 125

    G 117

    H 115

    J 107

5. $\begin{array}{r} 70 \\ \times 8 \end{array}$

    A 56

    B 540

    C 78

    D 560

6. $3\overline{)21}$

   F 7

   G 6

   H 63

   J 4

Part 3 Applications

7. Amanda went to the gym to work out.
   She ran on the treadmill for 25 minutes.
   She lifted weights for 15 minutes.
   Then she swam for 40 minutes. How
   many minutes did Amanda workout at
   the gym?

   A 65   C 80

   B 90   D 85

8. Miguel's grocery bill was $63.49. He
   paid with $80.00. How much money
   did Miguel get back?

   F $17.61   H $6.49

   G $16.51   J $16.41

9. There are 45 rubber bands in each
   package. Jerri bought three packages.
   How many rubber bands did Jerri buy?

   A 115   C 135

   B 225   D 270

10. There are 32 desks in a class. The desks
    are arranged into four equal rows.
    How many desks are in each row?

    F 9   H 128

    G 8   J 6

ANSWER ROW   1 Ⓐ Ⓑ Ⓒ Ⓓ   3 Ⓐ Ⓑ Ⓒ Ⓓ   5 Ⓐ Ⓑ Ⓒ Ⓓ   7 Ⓐ Ⓑ Ⓒ Ⓓ   9 Ⓐ Ⓑ Ⓒ Ⓓ
             2 Ⓕ Ⓖ Ⓗ Ⓙ   4 Ⓕ Ⓖ Ⓗ Ⓙ   6 Ⓕ Ⓖ Ⓗ Ⓙ   8 Ⓕ Ⓖ Ⓗ Ⓙ   10 Ⓕ Ⓖ Ⓗ Ⓙ

Work each problem.
Find the correct answer.
Mark the space for the answer.

Part 1 Concepts

1. What symbol correctly completes the number sentence below?

18 ☐ 3 = 15

A +

B −

C ×

D ÷

2. Which problem has an even answer?

F 5 × 9

G 37 + 42

H 65 − 12

J 72 ÷ 9

Part 2 Computation

3.   56
     +46

A 102

B 106

C 92

D 10

4. $16.02
     − 7.81

F $9.21

G $23.83

H $8.83

J $8.21

5. 39
     ×3

A 72

B 117

C 97

D 42

6. 6) 42

F 6

G 7

H 8

J 9

Part 3 Applications

7. Carlos collects postcards from places he visits. He had 53 cards in his collection. Last week he went on vacation and brought home 9 more postcards. How many postcards does Carlos have now?

A 62   C 63

B 44   D 72

8. Adam has $115.60 to buy a new stereo. Which of the following amounts can Adam spend on a stereo?

F $116.85   H $129.05

G $125.20   J $109.65

9. Elizabeth is making oatmeal cookies. Each batch makes 24 cookies. If Elizabeth makes three batches, how many cookies will she make?

A 57   C 72

B 27   D 8

10. Tessa collects baseball cards. She has 54 cards. She wants to put them in containers that hold 6 cards each. How many containers does she need?

F 6   H 7

G 8   J 9

ANSWER ROW **1** Ⓐ Ⓑ Ⓒ Ⓓ   **3** Ⓐ Ⓑ Ⓒ Ⓓ   **5** Ⓐ Ⓑ Ⓒ Ⓓ   **7** Ⓐ Ⓑ Ⓒ Ⓓ   **9** Ⓐ Ⓑ Ⓒ Ⓓ

　　　　　　　　2 Ⓕ Ⓖ Ⓗ Ⓙ   **4** Ⓕ Ⓖ Ⓗ Ⓙ   **6** Ⓕ Ⓖ Ⓗ Ⓙ   **8** Ⓕ Ⓖ Ⓗ Ⓙ   **10** Ⓕ Ⓖ Ⓗ Ⓙ

NAME _____

Work each problem.
Find the correct answer.
Mark the space for the answer.

Part 1 Concepts

1. Which number has a 2 in the thousands place?

   A 26,095

   B 15,023

   C 38,214

   D 42,157

2. XXXIII = ___

   F 23

   G 33

   H 18

   J 27

3. Which is the best estimate for the length of a key?

   A 2 centimeters

   B 6 centimeters

   C 15 centimeters

   D 40 centimeters

Part 2 Computation

4.   370
     −164

   F 106

   G 214

   H 206

   J 204

5.   73
    ×8

   A 564

   B 161

   C 581

   D 584

6. 9) 63

   F 5

   G 7

   H 9

   J 8

Part 3 Applications

7. The football team played two games this week. They scored 21 points in one game and 45 points in the other. How many points did the football team score this week?

   A 64   C 24

   B 66   D 76

8. Tiwa bought five posters at the souvenir shop. Each poster cost $7. How much money did Tiwa spend on all five posters?

   F $30   H $25

   G $35   J $42

9. Ben and six friends ordered some pizzas. There were a total of 28 pieces of pizza. How many pieces did each person get?

   A 2   C 4

   B 3   D 5

10. A bucket holds 7 liters of water. How many liters would eight buckets hold?

    F 15   H 56

    G 54   J 64

CUMULATIVE REVIEW

ANSWER ROW   **1** Ⓐ Ⓑ Ⓒ Ⓓ   **3** Ⓐ Ⓑ Ⓒ Ⓓ   **5** Ⓐ Ⓑ Ⓒ Ⓓ   **7** Ⓐ Ⓑ Ⓒ Ⓓ   **9** Ⓐ Ⓑ Ⓒ Ⓓ

              2 Ⓕ Ⓖ Ⓗ Ⓙ   **4** Ⓕ Ⓖ Ⓗ Ⓙ   **6** Ⓕ Ⓖ Ⓗ Ⓙ   **8** Ⓕ Ⓖ Ⓗ Ⓙ   **10** Ⓕ Ⓖ Ⓗ Ⓙ

NAME _____

Work each problem.
Find the correct answer.
Mark the space for the answer.

Part 1 Concepts

1. What number comes next in the pattern?

218, 198, 178, 158,

A 148

B 168

C 138

D 118

2. Which is the best estimate for the width of a ruler?

F 1 inch

G 5 inches

H 20 inches

J 50 inches

Part 2 Computation

3.

57	A 211
25	B 191
43	C 207
+ 86	D 223

4.

$13.50	F $15.58
− 2.08	G $11.42
	H $11.52
	J $10.62

5.

39	A 226
×7	B 213
	C 273
	D 286

6. $9\overline{)81}$

F 7

G 8

H 9

J 11

Part 3 Applications

7. Jacob weighs 67 pounds. Juan weighs 74 pounds. If both Jacob and Juan stand on a scale at the same time, what would be their combined weight?

A 137 pounds   C 131 pounds

B 141 pounds   D 153 pounds

8. There are six seating sections in the school auditorium. There are 84 seats in each section. How many seats are in the auditorium?

F 512   H 150

G 484   J 504

9. Shontay read a 91-page book in one week. She read the same number of pages each of the seven days. How many pages did Shontay read each day?

A 30   C 13

B 15   D 11

10. Brittany is 4 feet tall. How many inches tall is Brittany?

F 36   H 52

G 48   J 60

ANSWER ROW **1** Ⓐ Ⓑ Ⓒ Ⓓ   **3** Ⓐ Ⓑ Ⓒ Ⓓ   **5** Ⓐ Ⓑ Ⓒ Ⓓ   **7** Ⓐ Ⓑ Ⓒ Ⓓ   **9** Ⓐ Ⓑ Ⓒ Ⓓ

 2 Ⓕ Ⓖ Ⓗ Ⓙ   **4** Ⓕ Ⓖ Ⓗ Ⓙ   **6** Ⓕ Ⓖ Ⓗ Ⓙ   **8** Ⓕ Ⓖ Ⓗ Ⓙ   **10** Ⓕ Ⓖ Ⓗ Ⓙ

CHAPTER 15   CUMULATIVE REVIEW

Work each problem.
Find the correct answer.
Mark the space for the answer.

Part 1 Concepts

1. Which of the following problems has an odd answer?

A 275 − 133
B 43 × 7
C 54 + 37 + 85
D 20 ÷ 2

2. Which of the following fractions is equivalent to $\frac{2}{3}$?

F $\frac{2}{4}$ H $\frac{4}{6}$

G $\frac{3}{8}$ J $\frac{6}{10}$

Part 2 Computation

3.   76
      −28

A 48
B 104
C 58
D 44

4. 16 = ___

F VVI
G XIV
H XXI
J XVI

5. 81
      ×3

A 114
B 243
C 263
D 214

6. 9)54

F 4
G 5
H 6
J 7

Part 3 Applications

7. James is an author. Last week he wrote 83 pages. This week he wrote 57 pages. How many more pages did James write last week?

A 26   C 140
B 34   D 36

8. Melvin earned $12.50 helping his neighbor do yard work. He earned $17.25 helping his grandparents do yard work. How much did Melvin earn in all?

F $4.75   H $29.75
G $39.75   J $26.25

9. Lin worked three hours last week. How many minutes did Lin work last week?

A 300   C 180
B 120   D 160

10. While baby-sitting, Carli spent $\frac{1}{4}$ of the time doing a craft with the children. What fraction is equivalent to $\frac{1}{4}$?

F $\frac{2}{4}$ H $\frac{4}{8}$

G $\frac{3}{10}$ J $\frac{2}{8}$

CUMULATIVE REVIEW

ANSWER ROW   **1** Ⓐ Ⓑ Ⓒ Ⓓ   **3** Ⓐ Ⓑ Ⓒ Ⓓ   **5** Ⓐ Ⓑ Ⓒ Ⓓ   **7** Ⓐ Ⓑ Ⓒ Ⓓ   **9** Ⓐ Ⓑ Ⓒ Ⓓ
                    2 Ⓕ Ⓖ Ⓗ Ⓙ   **4** Ⓕ Ⓖ Ⓗ Ⓙ   **6** Ⓕ Ⓖ Ⓗ Ⓙ   **8** Ⓕ Ⓖ Ⓗ Ⓙ   **10** Ⓕ Ⓖ Ⓗ Ⓙ

Work each problem.
Find the correct answer.
Mark the space for the answer.

Part 1 Concepts

1. Which of the following fractions is equal to $\frac{1}{2}$?

A $\frac{1}{3}$ C $\frac{1}{5}$

B $\frac{2}{8}$ D $\frac{2}{4}$

2. Which of the following shapes has three sides?

F circle
G triangle
H rectangle
J square

Part 2 Computation

3. 18¢   A 63¢
     25¢   B 75¢
   + 30¢   C 73¢
          D 81¢

4. 43   F 387
   ×9   G 142
        H 362
        J 307

5. 6)48   A 4
            B 12
            C 6
            D 8

6. 3 ft = ___ inches   F 12
                         G 36
                         H 24
                         J 32

Part 3 Applications

7. There were 94 children and 13 adults that went on a field trip to a farm. How many people went on the field trip?

A 81   C 97
B 107   D 112

8. Mandy paid $18.35 for a CD. Juanita paid $12.89 for a CD. How much more money did Mandy spend on a CD than Juanita?

F $31.24   H $5.46
G $5.56   J $6.54

9. Mrs. Davis built a rectangular patio in her backyard. The patio is 8 yards by 9 yards. What is the area of the patio?

A 17 square yards
B 34 square yards
C 63 square yards
D 72 square yards

10. Elsa has a rectangular garden in her backyard. It is 13 feet long and 8 feet wide. What is the perimeter of Elsa's garden?

F 42 feet   H 54 feet
G 104 feet J 21 feet

GO

ANSWER ROW
1 Ⓐ Ⓑ Ⓒ Ⓓ   3 Ⓐ Ⓑ Ⓒ Ⓓ   5 Ⓐ Ⓑ Ⓒ Ⓓ   7 Ⓐ Ⓑ Ⓒ Ⓓ   9 Ⓐ Ⓑ Ⓒ Ⓓ
2 Ⓕ Ⓖ Ⓗ Ⓙ   4 Ⓕ Ⓖ Ⓗ Ⓙ   6 Ⓕ Ⓖ Ⓗ Ⓙ   8 Ⓕ Ⓖ Ⓗ Ⓙ   10 Ⓕ Ⓖ Ⓗ Ⓙ

CHAPTER 17 CUMULATIVE REVIEW

Work each problem.
Find the correct answer.
Mark the space for the answer.

Part 1 Concepts

1. Which completes the number sentence
7 □ 8 = 56?

A ×   C ÷
B +   D −

2. Which figure has six square faces?

F cylinder
G pyramid
H sphere
J cube

Part 2 Computation

3. 780
     506
  +392

A 1,768
B 1,576
C 1,678
D 1,278

4. 87
  ×5

F 142
G 407
H 435
J 335

5. 6) 36

A 5
B 6
C 4
D 12

6. 4 days = ___ hours

F 24   H 72
G 84   J 96

Part 3 Applications

7. An airplane has 265 seats. There are 67 empty seats. How many seats on the airplane are occupied?

A 332   C 208
B 202   D 198

8. Alvin worked 35 hours last week. He worked 7 hours each day that he worked. How many days did Alvin work last week?

F 4   H 6
G 5   J 7

Use the graph to answer questions **9** and **10.**

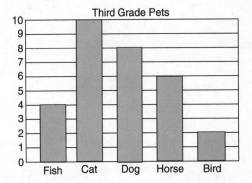

9. How many more children have cats than dogs?

A 4   C 1
B 3   D 2

10. How many fewer children have horses than dogs?

F 2   H 8
G 6   J 4

STOP

CUMULATIVE REVIEW

ANSWER ROW   **1** Ⓐ Ⓑ Ⓒ Ⓓ   **3** Ⓐ Ⓑ Ⓒ Ⓓ   **5** Ⓐ Ⓑ Ⓒ Ⓓ   **7** Ⓐ Ⓑ Ⓒ Ⓓ   **9** Ⓐ Ⓑ Ⓒ Ⓓ
                2 Ⓕ Ⓖ Ⓗ Ⓙ   **4** Ⓕ Ⓖ Ⓗ Ⓙ   **6** Ⓕ Ⓖ Ⓗ Ⓙ   **8** Ⓕ Ⓖ Ⓗ Ⓙ   **10** Ⓕ Ⓖ Ⓗ Ⓙ